Language Use in Interlingual Families

BILINGUAL EDUCATION AND BILINGUALISM
Series Editors: Professor Colin Baker, *University of Wales, Bangor, Wales, UK* and Professor Nancy H. Hornberger, *University of Pennsylvania, Philadelphia, USA*

Other Books in the Series

Please contact us for the latest book information:
Multilingual Matters, Frankfurt Lodge, Clevedon Hall,
Victoria Road, Clevedon, BS21 7HH, England
http://www.multilingual-matters.com

BILINGUAL EDUCATION AND BILINGUALISM 30
Series Editors: Colin Baker and Nancy H. Hornberger

Language Use in Interlingual Families

A Japanese–English Sociolinguistic Study

Masayo YAMAMOTO

MULTILINGUAL MATTERS LTD
Clevedon • Buffalo • Toronto • Sydney

To Jim, Pam, and JY
who have given me a rich, fulfilling, and fun life

Library of Congress Cataloging in Publication Data
Yamamoto, Masayo
Language Use in Interlingual Families: A Japanese–English Sociolinguistic
Study/Masayo Yamamoto.
Includes bibliographical references and index.
1. Bilingualism–Japan. 2. Family–Japan–Language. 3. Japanese language–Social
aspects. 4. English language–Social aspects–Japan. I. Title. II. Series.
P115.5.J3 Y36 2001
495.6'04221–dc21   2001030278

British Library Cataloguing in Publication Data
A catalogue entry for this book is available from the British Library.

ISBN 1-85359-540-3 (hbk)
ISBN 1-85359-539-X (pbk)

Multilingual Matters Ltd
UK: Frankfurt Lodge, Clevedon Hall, Victoria Road, Clevedon BS21 7HH.
USA: UTP, 2250 Military Road, Tonawanda, NY 14150, USA.
Canada: UTP, 5201 Dufferin Street, North York, Ontario M3H 5T8, Canada.
Australia: ootprint Books, Unit 4/92a Mona Vale Road, Mona Vale, NSW 2103, Australia.

Typeset by Florence Production Ltd.
Printed and bound in Great Britain by the Cromwell Press Ltd.

Contents

Acknowledgments

This book is a revised version of my doctoral dissertation submitted to International Christian University in Tokyo in 2000. Throughout the five years of juggling course requirements, dissertation writing, and my teaching commitments, I have received advice, encouragement, and support from many people.

First, I would like to express my sincere gratitude to my doctoral evaluation committee members at International Christian University: Prof. John C. Maher, my advisor, Prof. Peter B. McCagg, Prof. Yoko Kuriyama and Prof. Akira Tachikawa. I also wish to thank Prof. Randolph H. Thrasher, who was a committee member until his sabbatical leave. Without their valuable comments and suggestions, the dissertation would never have been completed. In particular, Prof. Maher offered me the most appropriate guidance and suggestions. His support in the warmest and the most gracious manner helped me continue the program. Prof. Steven J. Ross of Kwansei Gakuin University gave me invaluable help with the statistical analysis, enabling this study to go beyond mere description.

I am also greatly indebted to all the organizations and individuals, not named here in order to assure their privacy, who distributed my survey questionnaire, and to the families who took the time to fill it out and give many insightful comments. Although I was not able to include every family who offered themselves for follow-up interviews, I thank them for their willingness. Those whom I did interview all welcomed me to their homes or offices and shared their very private feelings about raising children and about bilingualism. One family even had the children cut classes to come home earlier, so that they could join the interview!

The questionnaire study which forms the basis for the dissertation was funded by a Japanese Ministry of Education Grant-in-Aid for Scientific Research (C), Project Number 07610517.

While the dissertation was still in progress, I made a presentation at the AILA 1999 conference in Tokyo, based on the same data. Prof. Annick De Houwer of the University of Antwerp gave me many encouraging comments and insights, which helped shape my dissertation.

I am very pleased and honored to be able to publish this revised version of my dissertation in the Multilingual Matters series, 'Bilingual Education and Bilingualism'. I would like to thank Ms Marjukka Grover of Multilingual Matters, for her enthusiasm and much valued assistance, and to Prof. Colin Baker for including this volume in the Bilingual Education and Bilingualism series. Also I am grateful to the anonymous reviewer for the support and many detailed comments and suggestions.

Lastly, my thanks go to my own family. My husband, Jim Swan, has always been willing to spare time to help me, both as a colleague and also as my best friend; without his help, support, and patience, I would not have been able to finish either the program or this book.

The original inspiration for all my studies was our children, Pam and JY, both now mature English–Japanese bilinguals with abilities in several other foreign languages, too. Watching them grow confirmed to me what an intriguing and rich experience it is to all of us – the children and the parents as well – to live in a bilingual environment.

Masayo YAMAMOTO

List of Symbols

Symbols Regarding People

pJ	: parent who is a native speaker of Japanese
pE	: parent who is a native speaker of English
pX	: parent who is a native speaker of non-Japanese
p_1	: parent–1
p_2	: parent–2
p_1cL, p_2cL	: parent who is a native speaker of the community language
p_1Y, p_2Y	: parent who is a native speaker of language-Y
p_2Z	: parent who is a native speaker of language-Z
M	: mother
mJ	: mother who is a native speaker of Japanese
mX	: mother who is a native speaker of language-X
F	: father
fJ	: father who is a native speaker of Japanese
fX	: father who is a native speaker of language-X
C	: child
C1	: first child (presence of sibling/s not specified)
C1-oc	: first child, without sibling/s (i.e. only child)
C1-sib	: first child, with sibling/s
C2	: second child
C3	: third child
C1-sib/C2/C3	: all children with sibling/s
C < 3 years old	: child younger than three years old
GM	: grandmother
GF	: grandfather
INT-1	: interlocutor 1
INT-2	: interlocutor 2
J–E bilinguals	: Japanese–English bilinguals

Symbols Regarding Languages

J	: Japanese language
E	: English language
X or Language-X	: non-Japanese language
Y	: language-Y
Z	: language-Z
B	: both of the given languages
pL	: parental language
cL	: community language

Symbols Regarding Language Interactions

$\Rightarrow$	: language use from speaker to addressee
pJ $\Rightarrow$ pE	: parent who is a native speaker of Japanese addressing parent who is a native speaker of English
pE $\Rightarrow$ pJ	: parent who is a native speaker of English addressing parent who is a native speaker of Japanese
pJ $\Rightarrow$ C	: parent who is a native speaker of Japanese addressing child
C $\Rightarrow$ pJ	: child addressing parent who is a native speaker of Japanese
pE $\Rightarrow$ C	: parent who is a native speaker of English addressing child
C $\Rightarrow$ pE	: child addressing parent who is a native speaker of English
$\rightleftarrows$	: speaking mutually
pJ $\rightleftarrows$ pX	: parents speaking mutually
pJ $\rightleftarrows$ C	: parent who is a native speaker of Japanese and child speaking mutually
pX $\rightleftarrows$ C	: parent who is a native speaker of non-Japanese and child speaking mutually
C $\rightleftarrows$ C	: children speaking mutually
1P-1L	: one parent–one language principle

Chapter 1
Introduction

In *interlingual families*, i.e. families with two or more languages involved, parents sometimes do not share the same language as their native language.[1] Such families have the potential to provide their children with a bilingual environment and, hence, with the opportunity to become bilingual in their parents' languages. Children may even acquire more than two languages as their native languages when their parents are bilingual themselves. Due to this potentiality, it is commonly believed that communication in such families is conducted bilingually in both parental languages and, thus, that children will naturally and spontaneously acquire both of the parents' native languages, just as monolingual children acquire their parents' shared native language as their own native language.

In spite of this general expectation, however, great variation is found in the degree to which this potentiality is actualized. Some families actively use both of the parental native languages, while others use only one, either voluntarily or involuntarily, and others use neither. Likewise, some children actually grow up to be active[2] bilinguals, attaining an active command of both languages. Some children, on the other hand, become passive bilinguals, developing only passive abilities, and others even become monolingual in the language of the mainstream society, in spite of their parents' desire and efforts to raise them to be active bilinguals.

What causes such variation? Under what circumstances do some families choose to use both parents' languages while others use only one? Why do some children attain bilingual abilities while others do not? The present study investigates variation in language use and tries to identify factors which cause the variation – in other words, how languages are used in potential bilingual families and what factors affect language use, especially that of children.

There have been studies which try to identify such factors, highlighting the dynamics of bilingual use in interlingual families (see the review of previous studies in Chapter 2). However, there seems to be some terminological and typological discrepancy in identifying subject families among these studies. Sometimes different terms are used to refer to groups of families with similar language background while the same terms are employed to refer to different groups defined according to different criteria. As a result, it is possible that conclusions drawn from findings in one study may not be applicable to subject families in other studies.

In the present book, I first review studies of interlingual families, highlighting the dynamics of language use among the family members and children's bilingual development. Secondly, I discuss terminological problems in research on interlingual families and propose a taxonomy of interlingual families, with which research findings can be most appropriately interpreted and applied.

Then, I present the results of a survey regarding how languages are used in Japanese–English interlingual families in Japan. First, using data collected with a questionnaire survey, I try to capture the linguistic milieu of such families residing in Japan, by describing their familial background, language use, attitudes and perceptions about bilingualism, and their efforts in promoting bilingualism in their children.

Next, I analyze how the languages are used among family members and what factors influence the children's language use. Factors considered include the languages spoken to the children by the parents, the languages spoken among the siblings, the languages used as the medium of formal instruction, the gender of the speaker of each language, and parental perceptions of bilingualism.

Lastly, I report the results of follow-up interviews conducted with a small number of families drawn from the sample, each representing a particular type of familial language use. Conducted approximately two years after the time of the questionnaire survey, the interview study was intended to obtain a more detailed, in-depth insight into each family's linguistic situation and to examine changes in their language use as children grow up: a focus on the dynamic aspect of familial language use.

Research on interlingual families is still scarce and there is much yet to be studied. It is hoped that findings in the present study will enhance our further understanding of bilingualism.

Notes

1. While some scholars treat the terms *native language* and *mother tongue* distinctively (e.g. Pattayanak, 1998: 130), others use them interchangeably (e.g. Crystal, 1991: 230). The present study treats both terms as interchangeable.
2. There are two pairs of dichotic terms commonly used to characterize bilingual abilities. In this book, whenever possible I prefer *active* to *productive* and prefer *passive* to *receptive*.

Chapter 2
Studies of Bilingualism in Interlingual Families

Previous studies investigating bilingualism in interlingual families may be grouped together under two major traditions: the linguistic and the sociolinguistic/sociocultural.

Studies in the linguistic tradition primarily examine how bilinguals acquire two languages by focusing on selected linguistic items – phonetic, phonological, morphological, semantic, syntactic – or how they employ those features in their utterances. One of the most detailed and often-cited studies in the linguistic tradition is that of Leopold (1970, 1978), which described in detail the process of the child's phonological, lexical, and syntactic development in German and English. Celce-Murcia (1978) observed in her study of the phonological and lexical development of an English–French bilingual child that the child's lexical choices seemed to be affected by the phonological difficulty of words: the child avoided words with sounds which are difficult to pronounce.

In regard to the early syntax of bilinguals, Deuchar and Quay (1998), using data from an English–Spanish bilingual infant, argue that, among bilinguals in the early stage, mixed utterances are mostly due to limited lexical resources, not due to a single initial system. De Houwer (1990) found that her young English–Dutch bilingual subject acquired morpho-syntactic features of the two languages independently and also in the same fashion as monolingual children of each language. Volterra and Taeschner (1978) and Taeschner (1983) analyzed the language acquisition process of young Italian–German bilingual children and proposed a three-stage process that bilingual children undergo in sorting out their two linguistic systems.

Studies in the sociolinguistic/sociocultural tradition, on the other hand, highlight the dynamics of bilingual development or use. Such studies generally try to identify factors that promote or hinder bilingual development or use, which affect the maintenance of, or shift from, a minority-status language. Since the present study is in the sociolinguistic/sociocultural tradition, I will first review at some length several major studies in this tradition and try to recapitulate salient factors found in those studies. Then, I will report the findings of previous survey studies on language use in interlingual families in the Japanese context.

Studies in the Sociolinguistic/Sociocultural Tradition

Döpke (1992a)

The main objective of Döpke's study (1992a and preliminary report of 1986) was to identify factors affecting the development of children's bilingual proficiencies, active and passive bilingualism. Döpke conducted case studies of six young children (2:4–2:8) who had been raised in an English–German speaking household, according to the one parent–one language principle[1] with each parent using only one of the languages. Her analysis suggested that among the factors influencing the promotion of bilingualism are the quantity and quality of linguistic input, parental interactional style, parental insistence on the minority language, and the emotional compatibility of the two languages.

Although Döpke places much more emphasis on the quality of linguistic input, in her view, both quality and quantity appear to be significant factors influencing the degree of bilingual development. It is important for children to be extensively exposed to the minority-status language in order to develop productive ability in that language. Döpke points out that later-born children in interlingual families often become passive bilinguals rather than active bilinguals, and attributes this fact to the reduced input of the minority language those children receive, in comparison to that received by their older siblings. Döpke also notes that the majority language is usually used for communication among siblings.

Regarding the qualitative aspect, Döpke suggests that productive proficiency in the minority language is developed when the minority language-speaking parent provides richer and more conducive linguistic input and also employs more teaching-oriented linguistic input than the majority language-speaking parent does. By 'teaching-oriented input' she means techniques such as paraphrasing, elaboration, expansion, and so forth. She also found it important for weaker-language parents to provide their children with more structurally-tailored input.

Another factor is a child-centred interactional style. Döpke found that her subject children conversed more frequently with parents who were more child-centred in their verbal interaction, and this enhanced inter-action promoted active bilingualism. Related to this, the emotional compatibility of the two languages was also considered influential. If children have satisfying experiences in both languages through inter-acting with their parents, Döpke surmised, they are more likely to use both than if their experiences with one of the languages is less satis-fying. Döpke's data suggested that:

> the children acquired the minority language in those families where the interaction with the minority language-speaking parent was a generally rewarding experience for them. Where, however, the inter-action with the majority language-speaking parent proved to be more enjoyable for them than that with the minority language-speaking parent, the children were not interested in using the minority language actively. (1992a: 190)

For families which adopt the one parent–one language principle, 'consistent adherence' (p. 186) to the appropriate language choice in communication between parents and children in both directions was considered crucial to the child's active bilingual development. Döpke found that parents' insistence on the use of the minority language was correlated to its active acquisition by children. In her study, the parents whose children developed productive proficiency in German were using high-constraint insisting strategies, such as requests for translation and unspecified clarification requests which required the children to respond in the minority language.

On the other hand, passive bilingualism seemed to result when the same factors were relatively lacking or less in effect in the minority language environment in comparison to the majority language environ-ment. Concerning linguistic input, for example, Döpke reports that 'where the majority language parent provided the more teaching oriented input, the children became receptive bilinguals only' (p. 191). She also argues that active bilingualism is hard to achieve when children lack sufficient and sufficiently varied contact with their minority language. The same result seemed to occur with the other factors as well.

Döpke also notes that resistance to use of the minority language was observed among some of the children after they learned that the minority language-speaking parents could understand the majority language. Such resistance is likely to lead to passive, rather than active, bilingualism or perhaps monolingualism.

Lastly, four years after the formal conclusion of her study, Döpke made an insightful observation that should be noted here. One of her most productively bilingual subjects, Fiona, 'continued to receive a rich and varied input in German' and 'never stopped speaking German. However, the beginning of school had its negative effects on the minority language even in this family: Fiona increasingly tried to speak English to her mother' (p. 194). This observation suggests that the language of formal instruction has a powerful degree of influence over the survival/ maintenance of children's abilities in the minority language (see also Wong Fillmore, 1991), although more recent research (see Winsler *et al.*, 1999) has suggested that, under certain conditions, this does not have to be the case.

Döpke (1998)

In her 1998 paper, Döpke strongly supports the one parent–one language principle to enhance successful attainment of active bilingualism in children. Criticisms of the principle as being elitist, unnatural, and its success being unpredictable she dismisses as 'largely short sighted' (p. 48).

Döpke takes the approach that the one parent–one language principle is a framework for language choice, not a strategy, and that this framework 'provides a macro-structure, which needs to be realized through micro-structure moves' (p. 49). This framework promotes various strategies constituting a continuum, with monolingual strategies at one end and bilingual strategies at the other. According to this approach, those who rigidly adhere to separated language use, strictly avoiding mixing and switching, are placed at the monolingual end, whereas those who separate their languages less rigidly are at the bilingual end.

Döpke tries to establish correlations between the location of the parental strategy on the continuum and the degree of bilingual competence their children can acquire. She claims that 'the further towards the bilingual [i.e. mixing] end of the continuum parents' strategies are, the less likely the child is to develop an active command of the minority language' (p. 50).

Döpke promotes the one parent–one language principle as creating the richest and most varied input possible for the demographically displaced dual-language families whose minority language is not supported in the society. When the minority language-speaking parent adheres to the minority language, s/he can (1) provide the child with the maximum quantity of exposure to the language; (2) ensure the child's exposure to the widest range of vocabulary and grammatical structures of the language through the full range of parent–child interactions in the language; (3) allow the language to develop appropriately with age, from simple to complex through natural interactions; and (4) detect underdeveloped areas of the language.

Lanza (1997)

Lanza investigated the language mixing of two young simultaneous bilinguals, Siri and Thomas. They were both 2-year-old Norwegian–English bilinguals in two families living in Norway, each with an American mother and a Norwegian father. In her detailed analysis of data derived from the longitudinal study of the two children, Lanza found that 'bilingual children as young as 2 years of age can and do use their languages in contextually sensitive ways' (p. 319) and young bilingual children are able to either differentiate two languages or mix them when the context is appropriate.

Her examination of the language mixing of these children indicated a certain relationship between the children's level of mixing and the parental discourse strategies towards the children's language mixing. On a continuum with the monolingual context at one end and the bilingual context at the other, Lanza identified five discourse strategies adopted by the parents: *Minimal Grasp Strategy*, *Expressed Guess Strategy*, *Adult Repetition*, *Move On Strategy*, and *Code-Switching*. At the most monolingual end of the continuum is the Minimal Grasp Strategy, in which the parent requests the child to clarify the utterance in another language, pretending not to understand what the child says. With this strategy the parent feigns the role of a monolingual and negotiates a monolingual context with the child. At the most bilingual end is Code-Switching, in which the parent incorporates the language that the child is using into her or his own utterance, making it a mixed utterance as well. With this strategy the parent proposes a bilingual context to the child. Between these two are: the Expressed Guess Strategy, in which the parent tries to reformulate the child's utterance in a form of yes–no question; Adult Repetition, in which the parent repeats the meaning of the child's utterance in the other language in a non-question form; and the Move On Strategy, in which the parent merely continues the conversation, indicating her or his comprehension of the child's utterance.

Lanza analyzed the children's mixing in relation to the strategies that their parents employed. Thomas had a strong preference for Norwegian over English and mixed both languages frequently in conversing with his American mother. Lanza found that Thomas' mother frequently employed the strategies towards the bilingual end, which indicates the mother's lack of attempts to negotiate a monolingual context. Under such circumstances, it was appropriate for Thomas to mix languages in interacting with his mother. On the other hand, Siri, though also dominant in Norwegian, did not mix languages with her mother as much as Thomas did with his mother. Unlike Thomas' mother, Siri's mother more actively negotiated a monolingual context by employing the strategies on the monolingual end. It is suggested that the mother's choice of strategies contributed to Siri's low level of mixing with her.

This analysis led Lanza to suggest that, given the child has limited access to the minority language, discourse strategies that the parents employ are decisive for establishing and maintaining the bilingualism of the child. Active bilingualism is more likely expected when the parent, especially the minority language-speaking parent employs discourse strategies which open negotiation of a monolingual context.

Hoffmann (1985)

Hoffmann (1985) reported the language acquisition of her trilingual children in Spanish, German, and English. From their birth, Hoffmann spoke to the children in German, which was the strongest language among those at her own disposal, and the father spoke to them in Spanish, his native language. The family was living in England; thus, though the parents did not speak English at home, the children were also exposed to English through their social contacts. At the time the article was written, both of their children were reported to possess trilingual abilities, being most proficient in English and less so in the other two languages, with some grammatical and stylistic shortcomings, but none the less competent enough to conduct daily communication in all three.

Through her observations as well as her experiences as the active provider of the German language input, Hoffmann suggests several factors which may affect the multilingual development of children in interlingual families.

First of all, a rich linguistic environment is essential. Her children were exposed to Spanish-speaking people who 'talk a good deal, [and] take gregarious pleasure in conversational exchanges' (p. 489) and to a rich linguistic environment in German, provided with the mother's conscious efforts. Hoffmann also points out that her younger child's English dominance is partly due to the fact that he was exposed to the language from a variety of sources and from his earliest days as well. The message here seems to be that the more balanced the exposure to the languages in question, the better chances for multilingual abilities to develop.

Parental and societal support is also important for multilingual development, in Hoffmann's view. Unsuccessful cases, she argues, lacked parental and/or societal support. One of the supports that minority language parents may supply is to take their children back to their home countries, to let them see that children there speak the language to their parents. This usually applies to the parents whose language is not spoken in the immediate society.

Positive psychological support and a multi-ethnic/-cultural atmosphere in the surroundings are also significant. In her own experience, Hoffmann points out that 'understanding, tolerance and support from relatives, friends and teachers of the children, and the absence of negative attitudes towards their trilingualism have been very important' (p. 490). It is also important that children are aware of the fact that their multilingual development is approved, even admired and praised by people around them.

Another suggested factor is the existence of siblings, which may be viewed as either an advantage or disadvantage. Having siblings, especially older siblings, will increase the opportunities for (younger) children to be exposed to a language which is not spoken at home, that is, the language spoken at school and/or in the immediate community. On one hand, this may enhance multilingual development if the language(s) spoken at home differ(s) from the one outside, as in the Hoffmann's case. It may be counter-productive, however, if the outside language is already used among the family members, at least as one of their languages. Siblings are often found to use either the language of school or neighborhood, and so it was in Hoffmann's case, resulting in more exposure to the outside language and less to the home languages.

Hoffmann highlights the pattern of language use by parents as an influencing factor, as does Döpke. However, they differ in regards to what pattern should be taken. While Döpke supports the one parent–one language principle, to enhance the children's development of bilingual abilities and also to maintain them, Hoffmann claims that both parents should use only a language different from the societal one. She states that if one of the parents uses the language of the society in addition to her/his native language, children will tend to achieve bilingualism but not to be able to maintain it.

Harding and Riley (1986)

In comparison to the studies of Döpke and Hoffman, Harding and Riley's work (1986) is less academic. It is actually more like advice to parents who are considering raising their children to be bilingual. Due to their lack of academic references, probably in order to make their work accessible to people unfamiliar with the issues, some of their assertions must be taken with caution, but they are suggestive none the less. Support for these assertions is provided from the authors' own experiences as well as from observations made in their many case studies.

One of the factors which Harding and Riley assert influences children's bilingualism is the amount of exposure to the languages to be acquired. Their basic principle is expressed in the form of a quasi-mathematical formula: '[l]earning is the product of "motivation × opportunity"' (p. 20). The more children are exposed to and use a language, the more proficient they will become. They make a point of emphasizing that those successful case studies often reported in literature are not just 'the luck of the draw,' but a consequence of the time and effort that parents put into interacting with their children.

Parental attitude towards their own languages is also considered to be a significant factor. If parents place little importance on their own languages, they are not likely to take much time nor make special effort to provide their children with language exposure.

In the authors' view, another important factor is the relative prestige of the two languages. They maintain that what makes the difference in a child's degree of bilingual attainment is not the degree of structural difference between the languages in question, but the relative social status of the two. Moreover, they assert that differences in status between languages influence the pattern of language use by parents. Languages such as English, French, and Spanish, as well as Hebrew and Arabic, are cited as prestigious.

Family mobility from one linguistic environment to another is also considered to affect the patterns of language use that parents take. They report an interlingual family which, due to the father's job, moved around from one country to another and was exposed to various languages. In such 'complicated' linguistic environments, the parents chose to make a monolingual home, speaking only the father's native language, in order to provide their children with a solid language base.

Another factor is the need for communication with the extended family. When parents want their children to keep close contact with minority language-speaking relatives, they are more inclined to speak the minority language to their children. It is often reported by parents that their passive bilingual children acquire some productive ability in the minority language after spending time with relatives.

Pauwels (1985)

That the pattern of language use, especially that of the parent addressing the child, is an influential factor in children's bilingual development and maintenance has been reported in previous research (i.e. the studies by Döpke and Hoffmann), but neither the patterns themselves nor the factors which comprise them have been fully investigated. One of the few studies to attempt such an investigation is Pauwels' (1985), which examined patterns of language use by Dutch-born migrants in Australia

Her study involved three different marriage forms: intra-ethnic between two Dutch-born partners (G1); inter-ethnic between Dutch and Anglo-Australian partners (G2); and inter-ethnic between Dutch and non-Anglo-Australian partners (G3). Sixty informants, 20 from each group, were randomly chosen from a pool of 250 candidates and were interviewed in regards to their language use.

Pauwels found that both inter-ethnic marriage types strongly affect the pattern of language use in a family, especially the language use of the Dutch spouse and the couple's children, in a negative way for Dutch maintenance. While Dutch is spoken by the Dutch spouse almost exclusively in speaking to her/his parents (100% in G2 and 95% in G3), it is used much less frequently in communicating with the non-Dutch spouse (20% in G2 and 15% in G3), and almost negligibly spoken to the children (10% in G2 and 5% in G3). Pauwels claims that the children in these inter-ethnic families are almost completely monolingual in English and that '[t]he L1 of their parents is neither understood nor spoken by them' (p. 54).

Although it is often assumed that the language shift of immigrant families takes three generations to complete (e.g. Appel & Muysken, 1987), from the findings in her study Pauwels foresees the complete language shift of the inter-ethnic families taking place with the first generation's passing. Language maintenance may be enhanced by being considered a part of the core value system (Smolicz, 1981); Pauwels attributes the accelerated shift in her subjects to the fact that Dutch residents in Australia discount it.

In investigating the differences in maintenance of Dutch by gender, Pauwels found that Dutch women married to Anglo-Australians maintained the language slightly better than their male counterparts did. She tries to explain the difference by the fact that, compared to the men, Dutch women seek more *gezelligheid*, i.e. social togetherness with other Dutch-speakers, which gives them more chances to speak Dutch.

Clyne and Kipp (1997)

Although their study did not focus exclusively on inter-ethnic families, Clyne and Kipp (1997) investigated shifts in home language use in Australia, based on three sets of census statistics. From their analysis, Clyne and Kipp identified several factors influencing language shift or maintenance: from the sociocultural standpoint, cultural distance, central core values, and ethnolinguistic vitality; from the demographic viewpoint, the relative population concentration of ethnolinguistic groups; and from the sociopolitical perspective, governmental language policies.

As another relevant factor, Clyne and Kipp also suggested increased contact with the majority society. They found that, in general, among children of some ethnolinguistic groups, language shift accelerates upon entering school or during the school years. The time when children enter the labor force or become independent from their family seems to be another period of increased language shift.

As did Pauwels (1985), Clyne and Kipp also found *exogamy*, i.e. marriage between spouses of different countries, to be a factor promoting language shift at home. It is reported that the rates of language shift tend to be higher in exogamous marriages than in *endogamous* ones (i.e. a marriage with both spouses born in the same country), due to the fact that in the former situation the non-English-speaking spouse lacks a speaking partner at home. Moreover, it was also found that in exogamous families across the board, a shift to English in the second generation occurs more when the parent of non-Australian background is the father rather than the mother.

Related to the last finding, there seems to be some correlation between parental gender and language maintenance/shift. Among first generation immigrants, men reportedly tend to shift more than women do; this was also found in Clyne's (1991) previous study.

Paulston (1994)

Paulston (1994) is another researcher who views the interlingual marital form itself as a factor leading to language shift. In identifying some causal factors in language shift and the maintenance of linguistic minorities in multilingual settings, Paulston claims that exogamy 'typically necessitates language shift for one partner, at least within the family' (p. 18), and the one who experiences the shift is usually of the linguistic minority group. She describes it as 'the most positive indicator of incipient shift' (p. 18). Endogamy, on the other hand, is viewed as a contributing factor to the retardation of language shift among linguistic minorities. Comparing the Italian and Greek communities in Pittsburgh, Pennsylvania, she cites more frequent endogamy among the Greeks to account for their relatively slower language shift.

Related to the marital form, Paulston points out that women frequently initiate language shift in choosing an exogamous marriage partner and in choosing the language used for child upbringing. This is often explained as a reflection of the gender power structure, with women, placed in a subordinate position in the society, being more sensitive to the language of power.

Other factors adduced by Paulston as affecting language shift/maintenance are the social prestige of the language and the individual's literacy in it. Distinct domains for each language, i.e. diglossic language use, is also mentioned as an influential factor in regards to language maintenance.

Lük (1986)

Lük (1986) investigated the ethnic identity and language use of children from mixed marriages of Hungarian and Slovenian ethnic backgrounds. The subjects were school-age children attending bilingual schools in Prekmurje, Austria. Out of the 61 children, 24 considered themselves ethnically Hungarian and the remaining 37, Slovene. Of the 24 children identifying themselves as Hungarian, 18 had a mother of Hungarian ethnicity, and 27 of the 37 declaring themselves as Slovene had a mother of Slovene ethnicity. From this fact, Lük concludes that children predominantly adopt the ethnic affiliation of their mothers in determining their own ethnic identity.

In the selection of languages at home, these children tended to choose the native language of their mother. Of the children claiming Hungarian ethnic identity, 75% had a Hungarian mother and a Slovenian father; 71% of that sub-group selected Hungarian in communicating with their mother, while only 24% chose Slovenian in speaking with their Slovenian father. Although less marked than in the Hungarian group, the children claiming Slovene ethnicity also seemed to show a tendency to choose their mother's language: 73% of that sub-group had a mother of Slovene ethnicity and a Hungarian father, and 51% of them used Slovenian with their mother but only 22% spoke to their father in his native language.

Among the children of Hungarian ethnic identity, Hungarian was frequently (60%) the language used in speaking among siblings. On the other hand, sibling interactions among the children in the Slovenian group used both Slovenian and Hungarian as often as they used Slovenian exclusively.

Harrison and Piette (1980)

Harrison and Piette (1980) analyzed data derived from three sources: their observations of some Welsh–English bilingual children, interviews with mothers of potential Welsh–English bilinguals, and cases reported by other researchers. They emphasize that social and psychological factors influence language choices by bilingual children as well as adults.

From the children's point of view, according to Harrison and Piette, language choice is the 'pragmatic manipulation of the resources' at their disposal (p. 229). By choosing the appropriate language for each particular setting, they try to catch the attention of adults they are interacting with, so that they can achieve their goals. Harrison and Piette describe an incident in which a 2-year-old French–English bilingual, who usually spoke to the researcher in English, switched to French in order to make the researcher play with her, thus successfully achieving her goal.

The language choice made by adults is also considered to be a factor influencing the child's own language use. Certain cultural and social norms seem to influence the language choice of parents, especially of mothers, and their language choice in turn affects the children's. In their 1977 study (quoted in Harrison & Piette, 1980) Harrison *et al.* found that, in a Welsh–English setting, middle-class mothers tended to raise monolingual English children, in comparison to mothers in other social classes.

They also acknowledged the influence of the father's attitude towards the given languages. None of the monolingual English fathers who discouraged speaking Welsh at home had bilingual children, while two-thirds of those who encouraged it did have bilingual children.

Lyon (1996)

Lyon's (1996) subjects consisted of both interlingual and non-interlingual groups, namely Welsh/English-speaking, Welsh-speaking, and English-speaking parents, in an area of North Wales where both Welsh and English are spoken.[2]

After analyzing the results of two questionnaire surveys and also recordings made of a small number of representative families selected from the whole subject group, Lyon enumerates several factors as influencing language choice in the family.

One of them is the father's language. Her findings suggest that wives appear to accommodate the main language of their husbands and this in turn sets the medium of communication at home. 'Fathers influence the language of the home' (p. 205). In addition to suggesting the possibility that women are better second language learners, Lyon perceives the father's language setting the language of the home as possibly a reflection of the gender power structure at home.

The language of the mother also plays an influential role in determining the language, not of the home, but of the child. In her stepwise multiple regression analyses of the data, Lyon found that the language of the mother accounted for 64% of the variance in the language that the child uses at three years of age. Lyon explained this as the natural result of mothers having very close relationships with their small children, spending a lot of time together, and having styles of speech appropriate to their children.

In Lyon's view, the language *per se* is also a contributing factor to the choice of language between a couple. The data show that more Welsh-speaking spouses use English to their English-speaking partners than vice versa.

Attitudes towards the particular languages involved and towards bilingualism itself may be other factors affecting what languages are used. Parental attitudes, along with societal attitudes, are likely to have a rather strong influence on the pattern of language use in the family. Lyon claims, however, that although the mere fact of parents having positive attitudes towards bilingualism is not enough to ensure children's bilingual development, a positive attitude combined with the mother's bilingual fluency improves the likelihood of the children's eventual bilingualism. The society placing a high value on bilingualism is another facilitating factor. Negative attitudes, on the other hand, greatly discourage bilingual acquisition.

It is worthy of note that, according to Lyon's study, the patterns of language use in interlingual families do not seem to predict a child's language development, whether monolingual or bilingual. Lyon did not find a direct relationship between them, and she stressed that the mere fact of being born into a family where both languages are spoken is not enough to ensure that the child will be bilingual at three years of age.

De Houwer (1999)

Some possible relationships of parental beliefs and attitudes to young children's active bilingual development are explored by De Houwer

(1999). According to a three-tiered framework she proposes, parental beliefs and attitudes are at the base of parental language choices and inter-action strategies, which strongly affect children's patterns of language use.

In her framework, parental attitudes include those towards a partic-ular language, towards bilingualism in general and early bilingualism in particular, and towards particular types of language choice (i.e. use of mixed utterances and inter-sentential code-switching). If parents have negative attitudes towards a particular language, they are likely to avoid using that language. Likewise, if parents have negative attitudes towards bilingualism, they are inclined to stick to one particular language in speaking to their children. And when parents are tolerant of children's mixed utterances, they may also mix languages in their own utterances.

Parental beliefs about the way children acquire language and the roles of parents in the acquisition process are also claimed to have substan-tial effects on parents' language behavior towards their children. Regarding parental beliefs, De Houwer introduces the notion of an 'impact belief,' which is 'the parental belief that parents can exercise some sort of control over their children's linguistic functioning' (p. 83). With a strong impact belief, parents think that their language use directly influences children's language use and their language learning. On the other hand, parents with a 'no impact' belief think that they have no control over children's linguistic functioning.

On examining findings from various studies on language acquisition of young bilingual children, De Houwer proposes the hypothesis that, in the family setting, sufficient support for the development of early active bilingualism is attained only in situations where parents not only have a positive attitude towards the languages involved as well as towards early child bilingualism itself, but also have an impact belief concerning their own roles in the language acquisition process. In other situations, insufficient support is received for the development of early active bilingualism.

Huls and Van de Mond (1992)

Huls and Van de Mond (1992) investigated language attrition in two immigrant Turkish families in the Netherlands. While the parents of both families were born in Turkey and migrated to the Netherlands, all of the children except one were born in the Netherlands. Since the parents in this study share the same single language as their native language, the language background of these subject families differ from most of the subject families in the studies previously reviewed. It is, however, worth reviewing their language use, too, especially in terms of the relationship between the children's language use at home and the mainstream language in the surrounding society. Besides, foreign-born parents in interlingual families share some characteristics with immigrant parents, after all.

The subject families of Huls and Van de Mond's study differ in the length of residence in their new homeland, with one family residing there for five years and the other family for 15. One of the main questions, which is relevant to the present study, is whether attrition is reflected in patterns of language choice among the family members.

According to Huls and Van de Mond's analysis, this is indeed the case. The length of residence in the host country is a determining factor for language choice. In general, the shorter the duration of residency, the more dominant the first language in the interactions among the family members, and, conversely, the longer the residency, the more dominant the second language.

Generational difference was also pointed out as a determining factor. When the language choices of each family member were compared, the children were found to favor Dutch more than their parents do. This was more so for the children in the family with the longer residency than for their shorter term counterparts. When the cross-generational interactions were reviewed, Turkish was often chosen in both directions, but with parents-to-children more often than children-to-parents, and also to a lesser extent for the family with the longer residency. However, the dominant language was clearly different in intra-generational interactions. Turkish was overwhelmingly dominant between the parents and Dutch was the preferred language among the children. The family members tended to mix the languages more often in cross-generational interactions than intra-generational ones, although the difference was not extensive. It also appeared that Turkish was used more often with emotionally-laden activities and conversational topics.

Summary

Each of the studies reviewed above differs in subjects, languages involved, or sociocultural background. However, the findings taken together suggest that children's bilingual development and children's language use are both influenced by factors in the linguistic environment as well as by sociocultural and familial factors.

The factors influencing the children's bilingual development and the families' language use can be summarized as follows (see Figure 2.1).

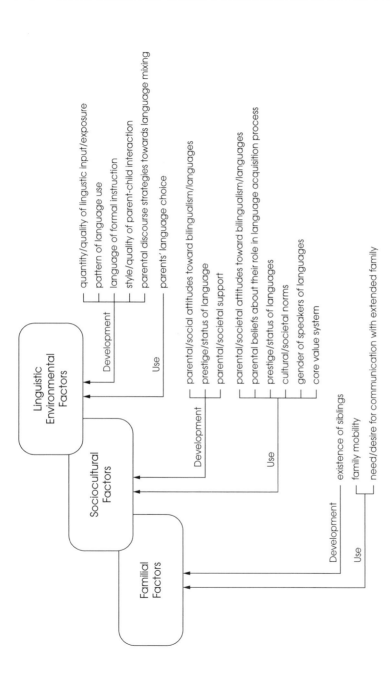

Figure 2.1 Factors influencing children's bilingual development and the families' language use: summary of the studies reviewed

Among the salient factors in the linguistic environment, those deemed influential to children's bilingual development are: the quantity and quality of exposure to the given languages (Döpke, 1992a); the pattern of language use by parents (Döpke, 1998; Hoffmann, 1985); the language of formal instruction (Döpke, 1992a); the style and quality of parent–child interaction (Döpke, 1992a); and parental discourse strategies towards child language mixing (Lanza, 1997). Parental language choice was found to have an effect on the children's language choice (Harrison & Piette, 1980) and to further their bilingual development (De Houwer, 1999).

Among the sociocultural factors found to influence parental language use and children's bilingual development, Lyon (1996) notes parental and societal attitudes towards bilingualism itself and towards the particular languages involved. Harding & Riley (1986) also consider parental attitude towards their own languages as an influential factor on children's bilingual development.

In addition to those attitudes, De Houwer (1999) also claims that parental beliefs regarding the way children acquire language and parents' role in the acquisition process affect parental language choices. Harding and Riley (1986) note that differences in status between the two languages may influence language use and bilingual development. Cultural and societal norms are also thought to influence parental language choice, especially that of mothers, and the mother's language choice in turn affects the children's language choice (Harrison & Piette, 1980). Another factor is the gender of the speaker of each language, with the father's language influencing that of the home (Lyon, 1996) and the mother's language influencing that of the child (Lük, 1986; Lyon, 1996). Language as a part of the core value system is claimed to affect parental language maintenance (Clyne & Kipp, 1997; Pauwels, 1985). Parental and societal support may affect the child's bilingual development (Hoffmann, 1985).

Familial factors include family mobility and the need or desire for communication with the extended family, both of which influence the parents' language use (Harding & Riley, 1986). Having siblings is thought to influence the bilingual development of children (Döpke, 1992a; Hoffmann, 1985).

It is significant to note that some of the studies (i.e. those of Clyne & Kipp, 1997; Paulston, 1994; and Pauwels, 1985) claim that interlingual marriage itself functions as a factor for promoting language shift among minority language-speaking families. It implies that among interlingual families, either the minority language is not used as frequently as the majority language, if ever, or that generational differences in language use exist.

Survey Studies of Interlingual Families in the Japanese Context

Very few studies have been conducted heretofore on the language situations of interlingual families in Japan, due to the fact that bilingualism/multilingualism is a relatively new area of investigation here. In this section I will first present the demographic background of the population of potential interlingual families residing in Japan. Then, I will briefly review the few existing studies and recapitulate their findings.

Demographic background

Approximately 99% of the whole population of Japan are holders of Japanese nationality (Statistics Bureau, Management and Coordination Agency, 1999) and most of them are also ethnic Japanese. The majority of them conduct their daily life mostly, if not exclusively, in Japanese. For these reasons, Japan has long been perceived as and described as a monolingual and ethnically homogeneous country by many mainstream Japanese, including scholars in language-related fields (e.g. Higuchi & Nakamura, 1978; Iritani, 1988; Oka, 1989; Suzuki, 1975; Toyama, 1974).

Actually, however, Japan has never been a genuinely monolingual or monoethnic country (Maher & Honna, 1994; Maher & Yashiro, 1995; Noguchi & Fotos, 2001). Though the number is not large relative to the mainstream Japanese, there have always existed several ethnic minority groups with their own separate and distinct languages: indigenous Ainus, Ryukyuans, Koreans, Chinese, and other 'foreign' people. Joining these 'older' groups are 'newcomers,' mainly consisting of people from Asian and South American countries, attracted by Japan's recent economic prosperity. Although the era of prosperity peaked in the mid-1980s, the number of registered foreigners continues to rise year after year (see Figure 2.2).

According to 1998 demographic statistics (Statistics Bureau, Management and Coordination Agency, 1999), of the total number of registered foreign nationals in Japan (n = 1,512,116), Asians comprise the largest group (n = 1,123,409: 74.3%), followed distantly by the South American group (n = 274,442: 18.1%). As of 1998, individual nationalities with over 10,000 members each were Korea (n = 638,828: 42.2%), China (n = 272,230: 18.0%), Brazil (n = 222,217: 14.7%), the Philippines (n = 105,308: 7.0%), the United States (n = 42,774: 2.8%), Peru (n = 41,317: 2.7%), Thailand (n = 23,562: 1.6%), Indonesia (n = 14,962: 1.0%), the United Kingdom (n = 14,762: 1.0%), and Vietnam (n = 13,505: 0.9%). Although the number of Koreans has always overwhelmed that of any other foreign

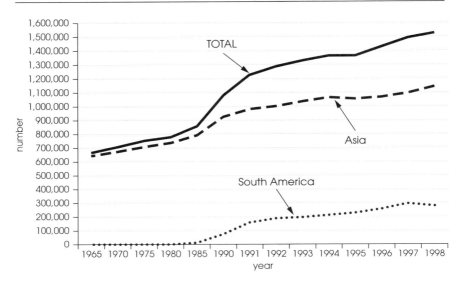

Figure 2.2 Number of registered foreign nationals (1965–1998)[3]. *Source*: Statistics Bureau, Management and Coordination Agency (1993, 1996, 1997, 1998, 1999)

nationality, their ratio to the total has been decreasing since around the 1980s (from 84.9% in 1980 to 42.2% in 1998) and, likewise, their absolute number has been gradually dropping since the peak year of 1990 (n = 687,940).

Being of an ethnic minority (e.g. an Ainu) or of a foreign nationality (e.g. a Korean) does not necessarily mean that the person speaks a language other than Japanese as her or his native language. Some members of these ethnic minority groups, especially among the older groups, may speak Japanese fluently and also regularly in daily life, and even as their sole native tongue (Kim, 1991; Yamamoto, 1996; Yim, 1993). Due to the inclusion of such cases, not every family categorized under the term *kokusai kekkon katei* ('families of international marriages,' in which only one parent is of Japanese nationality[4]) is necessarily interlingual.

Especially among the newcomers, however, some persons maintain their non-Japanese native languages and use them regularly in their daily life, either exclusively or complementarily to Japanese. Evidence for this claim may be found in the recent increase, following the 1990 revision of 'the Immigration Control and Refugee Recognition Act,' in the numbers of school-age children studying in public schools (from elemen-

Table 2.1 Native languages of children who need supplemental Japanese language instruction, 1991–1999

Native languages	1991	1993	1995	1997	1999
Portuguese	1,932	4,056	4,270	7,462	7,739
	(35.4%)	(38.8%)	(36.2%)	(43.1%)	(41.6%)
Chinese	1,624	3,171	3,908	5,333	5,674
	(29.7%)	(30.3%)	(33.1%)	(30.8%)	(30.5%)
Spanish	596	1,347	1,440	1,749	2,003
	(10.9%)	(12.9%)	(12.2%)	(10.1%)	(10.8%)
Filipino	121	284	503	618	854
	(2.2%)	(2.7%)	(4.3%)	(3.6%)	(4.6%)
Korean	326	328	373	482	499
	(6.0%)	(3.1%)	(3.2%)	(2.8%)	(2.7%)
Vietnamese	263	346	411	475	510
	(4.8%)	(3.3%)	(3.5%)	(2.7%)	(2.7%)
English	155	429	395	443	446
	(2.8%)	(4.1%)	(3.3%)	(2.6%)	(2.4%)
Others	446	489	506	734	860
	(8.2%)	(4.7%)	(4.3%)	(4.2%)	(4.6%)
Total number of children	5,463	10,450	11,806	17,296	18,585
	(100.0%)	(100.0%)	(100.0%)	(100.0%)	(100.0%)
Total number of native languages	43	48	46	53	58

Source: Ministry of Education, Science, Sports and Culture, 1992, 1994, 1996, 1998, 2000

tary to high school levels) who reportedly require supplemental Japanese language instruction. In response to this increase, the Ministry of Education, Science, Sports and Culture[5] (1992, 1994, 1996, 1998, 2000[6]) has been surveying their condition biannually since 1991 (see Table 2.1).

The survey results show that the number of such children has been steadily growing since 1991 and that it had more than tripled by 1999 (from 5,463 children in 1991 to 18,585 in 1999). Along with this increase in the numbers of the children, the variety of their native languages has also become more diverse. As of the 1999 survey, for example, while over 80% of the total number of 18,585 children speak as a native language one of the three major languages – Portuguese (7,739: 41.6%), Chinese (5,674: 30.5%) or Spanish (2,003: 10.8%) – the remaining children represent 55 other languages.

Although foreign children still comprise only a very small portion of the total number of school-age children in Japan, it is likely that the number will continue to rise, reflecting the steady increase of foreign residents.

Internationally married couples consisting of foreign nationals and Japanese are the main source of potentially interlingual families in Japan. The number of international marriages from 1965 to 1997, sorted by the nationality of the foreign spouses, are shown in Figure 2.3.

For most of the past three decades, marriages between Japanese and Korean nationals had been the most frequent. In 1991, however, the absolute number of Japanese–Korean marriages began to decrease (from 11,661 marriages in 1990 to 9,635 in 1991) and a year later was surpassed by that of marriages between Japanese and 'other,' which includes Filipinos, Thais, Brazilians, and Peruvians (10,508 Japanese–'other' marriages vs. 8,341 Japanese–Korean marriages in 1992). In 1997, the number of Japanese–Korean marriages was finally overtaken by that of Japanese–Chinese nationals (7,178 Japanese–Korean marriages vs. 7,464 Japanese–Chinese marriages), which is now the largest single pairing.

Along with the overall increase in the number of marriages between

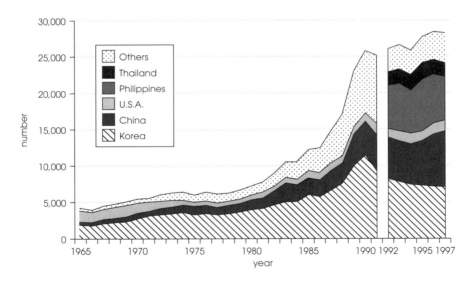

Figure 2.3 International marriages of Japanese and foreign nationals in Japan, 1965–1997, sorted by nationality of foreign spouse[7]. *Source:* Statistics and Information Department, Minister's Secretariat, Ministry of Health and Welfare (1999)

Japanese and foreign nationals, the number of children born of such marriages has been increasing. Reasonably, the demography of the child population mirrors the shift in the demography of the marriages. The demographic data on children born of Japanese and foreign parents from 1992 to 1997 indicate that, on the whole, there have been more children with a foreign mother than a foreign father. However, the proportions of foreign mothers or fathers vary greatly, depending on the nationality of the non-Japanese parent (Figure 2.4). The proportion of foreign parenthood, as of 1997, is best illustrated graphically in Figure 2.5.

Japanese men are more likely to father children of Filipino, Thai, Chinese, Brazilian, and Peruvian women (98.1%, 94.3%, 77.6%, 67.5%, and 56.9%, respectively). Japanese women, on the other hand, are more likely to bear the children of American or British men (89.1% and 79.1%, respectively).

The complementary nature of this distribution of spousal nationality by gender has profound implications for bilingual language acquisition in Japan. Although a person's nationality does not directly indicate native language, as is clearly seen in the case of Japan-born Koreans (Kim, 1991), the differences in proportions of foreign parenthood suggests that

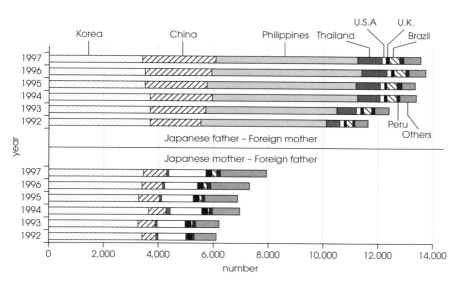

Figure 2.4 Births by non-Japanese parent's nationality (1992–1997). *Source*: Statistics and Information Department, Minister's Secretariat, Ministry of Health and Welfare (1994, 1995, 1996, 1997, 1998, 1999)

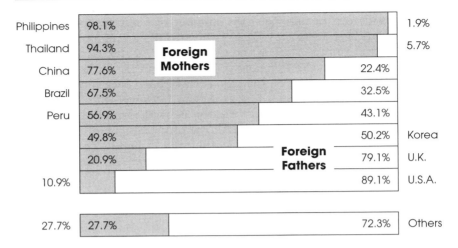

Figure 2.5 Proportion of foreign parenthood, 1997, sorted by nationality. *Source*: Statistics and Information Department, Minister's Secretariat, Ministry of Health and Welfare (1999)

the 'potential source' of the minority language in interlingual families – whether it is the mother or the father – differs greatly, depending on the nationality group, especially among the groups of 'newcomers.'

In addition to questions of societally more-esteemed or less-esteemed language, if, as Lyon (1996) and Lük (1986) found in their studies, the gender of the speaker of each language has some influence over parental language choice for this population, the pattern of language use at home may greatly differ, depending on nationality of the non-Japanese parent. Further, if parental language use affects children's bilingual development, as Hoffmann (1985) and Döpke (1998) found, then the probability of actualizing potential bilingual children's abilities may also differ, depending on nationality of the non-Japanese parent.

Yamamoto's 1985 survey (1985, 1987)

One of the very early studies of language use in interlingual families in Japan is a survey study conducted by Yamamoto in 1985 (1985, 1987). The subjects of the survey were interlingual families consisting of a parent who is a native speaker of Japanese (hereafter, pJ) and a parent who is a native speaker of English (hereafter, pE) with offspring. The survey results are found in Table 2.2.

Table 2.2 Yamamoto's 1985 survey results

Language(s) used	$pJ{\Rightarrow}pE$	$pE{\Rightarrow}pJ$	$pJ{\Rightarrow}C$	$pE{\Rightarrow}C$	$C{\Rightarrow}pJ$	$C{\Rightarrow}pE$	$C{\rightleftarrows}C$
Japanese	17	13	34	5	31	16	19
Both	15	14	15	16	10	15	2
English	21	26	6	34	4	14	3
Total	53	53	55	55	45	45	24

pJ: parent who is a native speaker of Japanese
pE: parent who is a native speaker of English
C: child (only children aged four or older are included in the analysis)
$\Rightarrow$: language use from speaker to addressee
$\rightleftarrows$: speaking mutually

The survey found that not only more pEs but also more pJs use only or mainly English in communication to their partner.

While parents tend to use the native language of one partner between them, each parent seems to prefer using her or his own native language in parent–child communication. That is, pJs most often choose Japanese and pEs most often select English in speaking to children. More children also tend to use Japanese in speaking to the pJ. However, that is not the case in child–pE communication. In speaking to the pE almost equal numbers of children choose English, Japanese, and both languages.

As for language use among siblings, it was found that most pairs chose Japanese as the main language of communication.

Oka's survey (1989)

Oka (1989) conducted a questionnaire survey to a small group (n = 20) of interlingual families consisting of one pJ and one parent who is a native speaker of non-Japanese (hereafter, pX) with offspring. Thirteen of his pX subjects were native speakers of English and the remaining seven were speakers of German, French, or Spanish.

As Table 2.3 shows, it was found that although the preferred language/s vary from one couple to another, each couple prefers to use the same language/s as a means of communication between them. That is, the language/s used by both partners match. The number of couples choosing language-X somewhat exceeds the number choosing Japanese and choosing both languages, but not by a wide margin.

Table 2.3 Oka's survey results

Language(s) used*	pJ ⇄ pX	pJ ⇄ C	pX ⇄ C
Japanese	5	18	3
Both	6	2	7
Language-X	9	0	10
Total	20	20	20

pJ: parent who is a native speaker of Japanese
pX: parent who is a native speaker of non-Japanese
C: child
Language-X: non-Japanese language
⇄: speaking mutually
* Both 'Japanese' and 'language-X' include 'dominantly Japanese' and 'dominantly language-X' respectively.

In regard to parent–child interactions, Japanese is overwhelmingly used between the pJ and children. On the other hand, language-X is more often chosen as the major means of communication between the pX and children, but again not by a wide margin.

Billings' survey (1990)

Billings (1990) investigated how languages are used in interlingual families and tried to determine what factors influence children's bilingual development. She analyzed data collected from a questionnaire survey of families consisting of one pJ and one pX with offspring. Native languages of the pXs include English, Chinese, Flemish, German, Hebrew, Italian, Korean, Portuguese, Spanish, and Swedish. The results of her study are found in Table 2.4.

Billings found three types of language use in her subject families: the one parent–one language principle; the home language strategy, where both parents use the minority language (= language-X); and a mixture of both languages. Her data show that more families employ the one parent–one language principle than the two other types.

Regarding the relationship between the parental language use to children and the children's bilingual proficiency, Billings (1990: 106) concludes that:

> the following intra-familial factors appear to have a positive significant relation to the development of children who are active bilinguals: 1) . . . , 2) using the one person, one language or home language strategy among the family members, and 3) . . . .

Table 2.4 Billings' survey results

pJ & $pX \Rightarrow C$	One parent–one language	Home language (Language-X)	Mixture of both languages
$(n = 30)$	19	6	5
Children's bilingual proficiency	⇓	⇓	⇓
active bilingualism	10	6	1
passive bilingualism	9	0	3
monolingualism	0	0	1

pJ: parent who is a native speaker of Japanese
pX: parent who is a native speaker of non-Japanese
C: child
Language-X: non-Japanese language
⇒: language use from speaker to addressee

For the cases in which the family reports using both languages, the data show that it tends to lead to passive bilingualism.

Her conclusion regarding the one parent–one language principle, however, is somewhat misleading. Of the six families employing the home language strategy, all report their children to be active bilinguals, while of the 19 families employing the one parent–one language principle, nine report their children to be passive bilinguals and ten families report their children to be active bilinguals. Thus, it seems to be more appropriate to conclude that the one parent–one language principle may lead to either active or passive bilingualism, while the home language strategy is more likely to promote active bilingualism.

Yamamoto's 1990 survey (1992, 1995)

Yamamoto (1992, 1995) conducted a second questionnaire survey of interlingual families consisting of one pJ and one pE with offspring. Many of the findings from the 1990 survey replicate those from Yamamoto's 1985 survey (see Table 2.5).

As found in the 1985 survey, more couples tend to use the same language/s mutually in communication with each other, and English is more often chosen. Likewise, both surveys found that both parents are apt to choose their own native language in speaking to their children. Children also prefer Japanese as a means of communication to the pJ.

Table 2.5 Yamamoto's 1990 survey results

| Language(s) used | | INT-1 INT-2 | INT-1 INT-2 | INT-1 INT-2 | INT-1 INT-2 |
by INT-1	by INT-2	$pJ \rightleftarrows pE$	$pJ \rightleftarrows C$	$pE \rightleftarrows C$	$C \rightleftarrows C$
Japanese	Japanese	10	10	1	7
Japanese	Both	4	0	0	0
Japanese	English	1	0	0	0
Both	Both	7	2	0	2
Both	Japanese	0	1	3	0
Both	English	6	2	0	0
English	English	23	2	12	4
English	Both	0	1	2	0
English	Japanese	0	0	0	0
Total		51	18	18	13

pJ: parent who is a native speaker of Japanese
pE: parent who is a native speaker of English
C: child (Only children aged four or older are included in the analysis)
INT-1: interlocutor 1   INT-2: interlocutor 2 $\rightleftarrows$: speaking mutually

Although not by as wide a margin as in the previous study, Japanese was also found to be most often chosen as a means of communication among siblings.

What differs from the findings in the previous study is children's language use in pE–child interactions. In the 1985 study, children almost equally chose English, Japanese, and both languages in speaking to the pE, but the 1990 study found that children use English most often in their communication to the pE.

Shang's survey (1997)

Shang (1997) investigated promoting factors of children's bilingualism with a questionnaire to families where at least one of the parents was a non-Japanese, but in some cases both parents were. For the purpose of comparison with the other studies reviewed here, I created Table 2.6 from Shang's raw data after excluding non-interlingual families (e.g. Cantonese–Cantonese) and interlingual families which did not include a Japanese speaker (e.g. English–Greek). The native languages of the pXs in the remaining families include English, Chinese, Dutch, French, German, Polish, and Spanish.

Table 2.6 Shang's survey results

Parental language use pJ & $pX \Rightarrow C$	One parent– one language	Home language (Language-X)	No particular strategy
(n = 43)	19	15	9
Parents' native languages	⇓	⇓	⇓
mJ-fX (n = 19)	11	3	5
mX-fJ (n = 24)	8	12	4
Language(s) used $pJ \rightleftarrows pX$	⇓ (n = 19)	⇓ (n = 15)	⇓ (n = 9)
Japanese Japanese	4	3	7
Language-X Language-X	10	11	1
Japanese Language-X	3	0	0
Both Both	2	0	0
Japanese Both	0	0	1
Both Japanese	0	1	0
$C \Rightarrow pJ$	(n = 37)	(n = 24)	(n = 19)
Japanese	36	5	19
Language-X	1	15	0
Both	0	4	0
$C \Rightarrow pX$	(n = 36)	(n = 24)	(n = 19)
Japanese	19	2	19
Language-X	16	19	0
Both	1	3	0
$C \rightleftarrows C$	(n = 30)	(n = 20)	(n = 16)
Japanese Japanese	29	3	16
Language-X Language-X	1	11	0
Both Both	0	6	0
Children's bilingual proficiency	(n = 36)	(n = 23)	(n = 19)
active bi-/tri-lingualism	26	18	1
passive bilingualism	10	3	10
monolingualism	0	2	8

pJ: parent who is a native speaker of Japanese   pX: parent who is a native speaker of non-Japanese   C: child   Language-X: non-Japanese language
➡: language use from speaker to addressee   ⇄: speaking mutually
mJ-fX: mother who is a native speaker of Japanese and father who is a native speaker of language-X   mX-fJ: mother who is a native speaker of language-X and father who is a native speaker of Japanese

Shang divided her subject families into three groups based on their parental language use to children: the one parent–one language principle, the minority language as the home language, and no particular strategy.

A few points bear mentioning. It seems that Shang included a family using the one parent–two language strategy among the first group, those ostensibly using the one parent–one language principle. Although no clear definition was given by Shang for the third group, no particular strategy, it seems that those who were not included in the other two groups were assigned to this group. Shang also included in the third group those who tried a strategy but failed early on. Shang tried to compare these three groups in regard to how languages are used among family members and the children's bilingual proficiency, as evaluated by their parents.

The data show that when speaking to their children, more parents employ the one parent–one language principle than any other. The next most favored strategy is the use of language-X. The use of the one parent–one language principle varies by pair combination. It is most often chosen by Japanese mother and language-X father couples (= mJ–fX), whereas use of language-X is most frequently employed among their counterparts, language-X mother and Japanese father couples (= mX–fJ). Even among the pairs of parents who adopt the one parent–one language principle to communicate with their children, use of language-X is most often employed in their communication to each other.

As for the children, they tend to use Japanese more than language-X in communication with their family members, except for those from the language-X families, who are apt to use language-X. Even among those families employing the one parent–one language principle, more children use Japanese rather than language-X in speaking to the pX. In the families with no specific strategy, none of the children use language-X.

Regarding the relationship between the parental language use to children and the children's bilingual proficiency, the data show that many more children are active bilinguals in the families where not only the one parent–one language principle but also use of language-X is employed. Shang implies that adopting a strategy for language use in the family increases the chances of promoting active bilingualism, while having no specific strategy is the least likely to promote it.

Summary

In addition to the fact that the sample sizes of all the subject groups were small, all the studies reviewed above differ in the variables under investigation, such as the languages involved, the range of the children's ages, or gender distribution of the speakers of the given languages among the subjects. Due to such limitations, I am fully aware that the findings derived from them are only tentative. None the less, I believe that the findings combined together provide us with useful suggestions for further investigation of language use in interlingual families. The findings from all the studies described are summarized in Table 2.7. The findings suggest that the parents in an interlingual family tend to choose the native language of one of them as the common language between them, and that the language chosen by more couples is language-X.

While the parents may employ monolingual language use between themselves, they seem to prefer the one parent–one language principle in addressing their children. In accordance with this finding, each parent reportedly tends to choose her/his own native language in communicating with children. This choice of language, however, is well-echoed only between the pJ and children. Children are found to choose Japanese most often in speaking to the pJ, but to the pX they often use Japanese as well as language-X or both languages. One study finds that children speak Japanese more often to the pX if the parents employ the one parent–one language principle.

Concerning parental language choice to their children, one study suggests that it may be affected by the gender of the native speakers of each language. It is claimed that couples consisting of a mother who is a native speaker of language-X and a father who is a native speaker of Japanese (= mX–fJ) tend to choose language-X, whereas their counterparts (mJ–fX) tend to adopt the one parent–one language principle.

More children tend to use Japanese in speaking to their siblings. It is also suggested that, except for those whose parents both use language-X, more children are inclined to choose Japanese in speaking to both of their parents as well as to their siblings. It is even reported that children whose parents do not employ any specific strategy strongly favor Japanese in speaking to other members of the family.

It has been suggested that exclusive use of language-X by both parents promotes the child's active bilingualism. The one parent–one language principle, on the other hand, seems to be more equivocal in its effect: either active or passive bilingualism may result. Further, when both languages are used, children tend to be only passive bilinguals. When parents do not employ any specific strategy in their language use, the lack of a defined goal may lead to either passive bilingualism or monolingualism, presumably in Japanese.

On the whole, it is strongly suggested that Japanese, the language of the mainstream society, has great influence over children's choice of

Table 2.7 Summary of research findings in the Japanese context to date

Language use		
pJ ⇄ pX	They tend to use the same language	Y-90/O
	They tend to use language-X	Y-85/Y-90/O/Sh
pJ & pX ⇒ C	1P-1L is most often chosen	Sh/Bl
	1P-1L is most often chosen among mJ-fX	Sh
	Language-X is most often chosen among mX-fJ	Sh
C ⇒ all family members	(Except for families using language-X) J is more often chosen	Sh
	(In families with no specific strategy) Language-X is never chosen	Sh
pJ ⇄ C	J is most often chosen	Y-90/O
pJ ⇒ C	J is most often chosen	Y-85
C ⇒ pJ	J is most often chosen	Y-85
pX ⇄ C	Language-X is most often chosen	Y-90/O
pX ⇒ C	Language-X is most often chosen	Y-85
C ⇒ pX	Language-X, J, and B are almost equally chosen	Y-85
	(Even among 1P-1L families) J is more often chosen	Sh
C ⇄ C	J is most often chosen	Y-85/Y-90
	(Except for families using language-X) J is most often chosen	Sh

Parental language use to children and their bilingual proficiency

Active bilingualism	• Use of language-X promotes active bilingualism	Bl
⇓	• Both 1P-1L and use of language-X increase the chances of promoting active bilingualism	Sh
⇓	• 1P-1L leads to either active or passive bilingualism	Bl-am
passive bilingualism		
⇓	• B tends to lead to passive bilingualism	Bl
⇓	• No specific strategy tends to produce passive bilingualism or monolingualism	Sh
Monolingualism		

Key: see p. 35

Table 2.7 (*continued*)

pJ: parent who is a native speaker of Japanese
pX: parent who is a native speaker of non-Japanese
C: child
J: Japanese language
Language-X: non-Japanese language
B: both of the given languages
➡: language use from speaker to addressee
⇄: speaking mutually
1P–1L: one parent–one language principle
mJ–fX: mother who is a native speaker of Japanese and father who is a native speaker of language-X
mX–fJ: mother who is a native speaker of language-X and father who is a native speaker of Japanese
Y-85: Yamamoto (1985, 1987)
O: Oka (1989)
Bl-am: Billings (1990), as amended by the present author
Y-90: Yamamoto (1992, 1995)
Sh: Shang (1997)

language. Children seem to favor Japanese over language-X, even when speaking to the pX who uses the latter. As far as familial language use is concerned, unless an exclusively language-X environment is provided by both parents, children are inclined to use Japanese more often and may develop only passive bilingualism, or perhaps monolingualism in Japanese.

Notes

1. This type of parental language use has been termed in various ways by different scholars: 'Ronjat's principle of one parent, one language' by Bain & Yu (1980), 'one person/one language principle' by De Houwer (1990), 'one person–one language method' by Romaine (1995), 'one person-one language approach' by Lyon (1996), or 'one person–one language strategy' by Lanza (1992). It even has been called differently by the same author at different times: 'one parent–one language principle' by Döpke (1992a) and 'one person–one language principle' by Döpke (1998). Because of the emphasis on child–parent interactions in the present study, this book employs Döpke's (1992a) term, 'one parent–one language principle,' except in the quotations where other terms were used by the original authors.
2. Due to her imprecise description of the subjects, it is not clear whether being 'a speaker of' any of these languages necessarily signifies being 'a native speaker.' The native/non-native status of a given language may affect its speaker's linguistic behavior in various ways. (This issue is discussed in Chapter 3.) If, as seems to be the case, her subjects here are the same as

those in her 1991 survey (Lyon & Ellis, 1991), they were reported to be divided strictly based on their language use, not on their culture or nationality. The native/non-native status of the languages, however, was not clearly delineated there, either, requiring substantial assumption.

3. The graph shows only the total number and the numbers of the two groups which made the most drastic increases since the mid-1980s, Asians and South Americans. Moreover, the total does not include visa overstayers (n = 284,744 as of 1 November 1995) (Japan Immigration Association, 1996).

4. Strictly speaking, marriages between partners of any two different nationalities should be considered *kokusai kekkon*. However, the Japanese term has conventionally been used in the restricted sense defined in the text.

5. Due to a 2001 reorganisation of the government ministries, the official (English) title is now the Ministry of Education, Culture, Sports, Science and Technology.

6. The first two surveys excluded high school students, but relative to the total the numbers were almost negligible: 264 students (2.2% of the total) in 1995 and 461 (2.7% of the total) in 1997. The 1999 survey also includes, for the first time, special schools for handicapped children.

7. As the graph before the breaking line shows, until 1991 Ministry of Health and Welfare (renamed in 2001 as the Ministry of Health, Labour and Welfare) records for marriages between Japanese and foreign nationals were categorized under only four groups: Korea, China, the USA, and 'other foreign countries.' Since 1992, however, the figures for five additional countries have become significant enough to be broken out of the 'other foreign countries' category, making a total of nine reported groups: Korea, China, the USA, the Philippines, Thailand, the UK, Brazil, Peru, and 'other foreign countries.' The values for the UK, Brazil, and Peru are too small to register on the graph, however, so in this book they continue to be combined with 'others.' The graph after the breaking line therefore specifies only the figures for the five largest individual groups (namely Korea, China, the USA, the Philippines, Thailand) and 'others,' into which the figures for all the remaining groups are combined.

Chapter 3
Taxonomy of Interlingual Family Types

Terminological Problems

Introducing and interpreting terms is risky, because the same term often refers to quite different entities or phenomena, due to the fact that terms are frequently defined differently from one scholar to another. Having various definitions may not in itself pose a problem. Instead, it may increase flexibility in usage of terms 'since in this way the researcher is able to choose the one [definition] that best suits her or his purpose' (Hoffmann, 1991: 18). This may be so as long as terms are clearly defined when they appear first time in any particular paper.

However, such is not always the case, especially when a particular definition of a certain term has earned a firm position as a general definition in the terminology of the field of study. In that case, the term may be regarded as self-explanatory and used without being expressly defined. If the term is then used to refer only to particular cases of entities or phenomena whose characteristics may be quite different from those of the rest, discrepancies can be easily overlooked.

One of the most conspicuous examples in the field of bilingualism studies may be the term *bilingual* itself. A bilingual may be generally defined as 'a person who knows and uses two languages' (Richards *et al.*, 1985: 28). This general definition covers the bilingual subjects in Yoshioka (1929) as well as those in Peal & Lambert (1962). However, the problem is clearly illustrated by the greatly contrasting findings and conclusions of these two studies.

The subjects in Yoshioka's study (1929) were English–Japanese 'bilingual' children, aged from 9 to 15 years, whose parents were mainly town merchants, farmers, and farm hands in California. Yoshioka provided no detailed data on the subjects' language abilities. From his rather general description of them, it can only be assumed that the younger subjects were probably dominant in English while the older ones were probably more balanced in both languages. Yoshioka compared the results of intelligence tests given to them with the American and Japanese age norms. Based on his findings, Yoshioka concluded that 'bilingualism in young children is a hardship and devoid of apparent advantage, because bilingualism appears to require a certain degree of mental maturation for its successful mastery' (Yoshioka, 1929: 479).

The subjects studied by Peal and Lambert (1962), on the other hand, were 10-year-old French–English 'bilinguals' and 10-year-old French monolinguals from French schools classified as middle-class schools in Canada. Peal and Lambert reported that their bilingual subjects were extremely carefully screened and only balanced bilinguals were selected for their study. They compared the results of the bilingual group and the monolingual group on intelligence tests and attitudinal measures. Their conclusions are that:

> bilinguals performed significantly better than monolinguals on both verbal and non-verbal intelligence tests. Several explanations are suggested as to why bilinguals have this general intellectual advantage. It is argued that they have a language asset, are more facile at concept formation, and have a greater mental flexibility. (Peal & Lambert, 1962: 22)

Regarding the putative influence of bilingualism on children's intelligence, extremely different pictures emerge from these two studies of 'bilingual' subjects, one very negative and the other very positive. Although both groups of subjects are categorized as 'bilingual,' they are different in their backgrounds. Thus, it is not clear whether mere bilingualism itself is responsible for the results of each study, or to what degree other socio-psychological, political, socio-economic, educational, attitudinal, ethno-cultural, or demographic factors are also responsible.

A contrasting problem is that similar subjects may sometimes be referred to by a variety of terms. Families with parents who have different native languages, such as are the subjects of the present study, have been referred to in various ways. Examples are *exogamy* (e.g. Pauwels, 1985), *mixed marriages* (e.g. Romaine, 1995; Schaerlaekens *et al.*, 1995), *mixed-language marriages* (e.g. Baker & Prys Jones, 1998), *cross-language marriages* (e.g. Lyon & Ellis, 1991), *dual-language couples* (e.g. Döpke, 1998), *ethnolinguistically mixed households* (e.g. Clyne, 1991), *exogamous families* (e.g. Clyne & Kipp, 1997), *mixed-lingual families* (e.g. Hamers & Blanc, 1989), and *bilingual families* (e.g. Döpke, 1992a; Evans, 1987; Harding & Riley, 1986; Lyon, 1996; Pan, 1995; Skutnabb-Kangas, 1981).

Compounding the confusion, these same terms are also sometimes used to refer to different kinds of subjects defined according to different criteria. The term *bilingual families*, for instance, is sometimes defined based on the status of the languages to their speakers (i.e. whether the given languages are their native languages or not) and sometimes on how the languages are used by the family members, regardless of status.

Skutnabb-Kangas (1981), for example, uses the status of the languages as a criterion, and defines *bilingual families* as those 'in which the parents have different mother tongues' (1981: 78). Despite this clear statement, however, she included Saunders (1982) as one of the cases in her study of bilingual families, a family in which the children were raised in German by their father, who is a native speaker of English, and in English by their mother, who is also a native speaker of English. To be precise, this case should not be considered a bilingual family under Skutnabb-Kangas' definition, since both parents share the same language, English, as their native language and 'the father is not a native speaker of German' (Saunders, 1982: 23).

Harding and Riley (1986), on the other hand, do not use the status of the languages as their criteria for defining bilingual families. In their review of the literature on bilingualism, they introduce five main types of bilingual families; in three of them, the parents have different native languages and in the remaining two, the parents share the same native language. What distinguishes the families in the latter two types from monolingual families is language use: in the first type, the parent's native language is different from the language they speak to the child, while in the second type, the language spoken among the family members is different from the language of the surrounding community.

Likewise, Döpke (1992a) does not consider the fact of parents having different native languages as a defining criterion. In her description of bilingual families adopting the 'one parent–one language' principle, she presents four types of families: (1) parents having different native tongues, one of which is the language of the wider community; (2) parents having different native tongues, neither of which is the language of the wider community; (3) both parents having the language of the wider community as their native tongue; and (4) both parents having the same minority language as their native tongue. The last two types are categorized as bilingual families only if one of the parents speaks to the child in a language other than her/his native tongue.

Neither does Lyon (1996) adopt language status as a criterion. She argues that the regular use of two or more languages is a minimum requirement for a family to be defined as bilingual. 'Regularity' in her definition, however, is very loosely construed. She includes even a family that usually uses one language in everyday life and the second language only once a week in church.

Another problem adding to the confusion is that the terms are sometimes used without an explicit definition, as if they were self-explanatory. Even when defined, the definitions sometimes lack any mention of language itself or of whether a particular language is native to the speakers in question. Often there is no way of knowing what language background the subjects are from. Pauwels (1985: 39), for example, explains:

> In an immigration context, exogamy refers to a marriage where the partners stem from different ethnic rather than religious backgrounds. Also relevant to a sociolinguistic investigation in Australia is the distinction between marriages in which both sides come from an ethnolinguistic background different from that of the indigenous population and/or that of the longest established settler group, and marriages in which one partner is a member of the latter group.

Clyne and Kipp (1997) have used birthplace as a criterion to classify families as endogamous. They clearly admit that birthplace is 'a not particularly satisfactory surrogate for "language of background"' (p. 462), but explain that this has to suffice, due to a lack of data regarding the native languages of the subjects.

Four Subcategories

The foregoing section demonstrates a clear need for unambiguous terminology. Confusion seems to arise partly from defining *interlingual families* (or similar, equivalent terms) according to different criteria. Some researchers define their subject families by parental native language, whereas other researchers focus on familial language use. In order to clarify this terminological confusion and make adequate comparisons possible among different research findings, I would like to propose a framework whereby interlingual families can be categorized consistently. To do so, the framework must be able to accommodate every possible family type, both those defined by parental native language and also those defined by language use.

I hasten to note, I am fully aware that the notion of *native speaker* has been criticized for its ambiguity as well as for its political implications (see Singh, 1998), and that it is sometimes difficult to determine which language is actually a person's native language, especially in case of bilingual populations (see Skutnabb-Kangas, 1981, 2000). None the less, we cannot rule out the possibility that whether or not a given language is at least perceived by its speaker as her or his native language affects her or him in various important ways. As Crystal (1997: 255), for instance, points out:

> [t]he implication is that [a native language], having been acquired naturally during childhood, is the one about which a speaker will have the most reliable INTUITIONS, and whose judgements [sic] about the way the language is used can therefore be trusted.

Further, from the neurolinguistic viewpoint, Paradis (1998) reports clear neurofunctional distinctions between a native speaker and a non-native speaker of a language. Some of the differences are found in the use of linguistic competence or metalinguistic knowledge, the extent to which speakers rely on right cerebral hemisphere-based pragmatic aspects of communication, or the cerebral mechanisms involved.

Differences are also observed at the affective level. Though acknowledging evidence for her claims to be anecdotal, Skutnabb-Kangas (1981: 49–50) maintains that:

> Many bilinguals testify to the fact that their second language, which they learnt later in life, feels colder, more alien, less rich in words, less subtle and on the whole poorer. It does not go as deep, it does not come as close to them, it does not affect them as strongly as the first. It feels more superficial, more 'stuck on', it does not awaken the same deep layers of the personality. One is more oneself in one's mother tongue. All this seems also to be true of many bilinguals who know their second language very well, just as well, or in many cases even better, than the language they learnt first.

It could be suggested that these potential differences have some influence over speakers' use of a given language as well as over the language use of the family as a whole. In a non-community language family, for instance, the community language may perhaps never be considered as a means of communication among the family members, if neither parent is a native speaker of that language and neither feels comfortable in it. On the other hand, the use of the community language may be greatly encouraged if one of the parents is a native speaker of that language and favors it over any other. Likewise, the community language may perhaps be favored by a child, despite parental efforts to promote another language, if the child is aware that both parents are native speakers of the community language.

Thus, it is important to explicitly identify the groups of interlingual families from which the subjects are drawn, and that is the reason why I propose the following analytical framework. By the first of my two proposed criteria, families can be categorized as *cross-native language,* in which parents have different native language backgrounds, or *shared-native language,* in which parents have the same native language background. By the second proposed criterion, families can be classified as either *community language,* in which parental native languages include the community language, or *non-community language,* in which neither/ none of the parental native languages is the community language. The resulting four categories are displayed in Figure 3.1:

(A) cross-native/community language families;
(B) cross-native/non-community language families;
(C) shared-native/community language families; and
(D) shared-native/non-community language families.

Families included in Group A, *cross-native/community language families,* are those in which the parents have different native languages (p_1cL and p_2Y), one of which (cL) is the major language of the community. Thus, the parental native languages and the community language partially match. Families in this group are interlingual by virtue of parental native language background. In the Japanese setting, families consisting of a parent who is a native speaker of Japanese and a parent who is a native speaker of non-Japanese would be included in this group.

The parents in Group B, *cross-native/non-community language families,* also are from different native language backgrounds (p_1Y and p_2Z), but neither of their languages is the same as the major language spoken in the community. The parental native languages and the community language totally mismatch. As in Group A, families in this group are interlingual by virtue of parental native language background. Likewise, in the Japanese setting, families included in this group would be those consisting of parents whose native languages are different from each other's and both non-Japanese.

Unlike parents in Groups A and B, those in Groups C and D have the same native language. The language of both parents (p_1cL and p_2cL) in Group C, *shared-native/community language families,* is identical to that of the community. In other words, the parental native language totally matches the community language. Unlike the two previous groups, these families must activate their bilingual potential by using another language among the family members. In the Japanese setting, families included in this group would be those consisting of two parents who are both

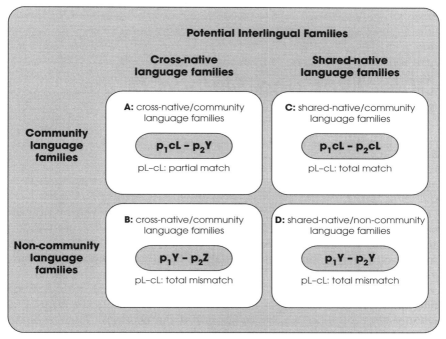

p₁: parent-1   p₁: parent-2
p₁cL, p₂cL: parent who is a native speaker of the community language
p₁Y, p₂Y: parent who is a native speaker of language-Y
p₂Z: parent who is a native speaker of language-Z
pL: parental language   cL: community language   Y: language-Y   Z: language-Z

Figure 3.1 Four types of interlingual families

native speakers of Japanese, but with another language being used at least partially for communication among the family members. Those who use Japanese as the sole means of communication are not classified as interlingual families.

On the other hand, the native language of the parents (p_1Y and p_2Y) in Group D, *shared-native/non-community language families*, is different from that of the community. The parental native language is a total mismatch with the community language. Families in this group are inter-lingual by virtue of the community language which surrounds them. In the Japanese setting, families included in this group would be those consisting of parents whose native languages are the same as each other's and both non-Japanese.

Chapter 4

Objectives and Method of the Present Study

Objectives

In the present study there are three major objectives. The first objective is to elucidate the language environments of cross-native/community language families living in Japan. This is done with responses to a questionnaire survey[1] of a group of cross-native/community language families.

The second objective is to analyze data obtained from the questionnaire to learn how languages are used among the family members and what factors influence the language use of the children. To investigate the above, two specific research questions are asked: (1) Who uses what languages to whom? and (2) Under what circumstances is a child likely to speak in the minority-status language to its native-speaking parent?

Regarding the first research question, a typological model of the patterns of language use in cross-native/community language families is formed. Using the model, patterns of language use of the subject families in the present study are categorized and some characteristics of the subjects are extracted.

While it is only natural that children being raised in monolingual families speak the same language as their parents, it is not necessarily the case with those in cross-native/community language families. While a mother speaks her native language to her children, for example, they may respond to her in their father's native language, or vice versa. What factors influence such children's language choices? The second research question – *Under what circumstances is a child likely to speak in the minority-status language to its native-speaking parent?* – is asked to examine relationships between children's choices of language and other variables. The relationship between a particular type of parental language use, namely the 'one parent–one language' principle, and the language use of children is also examined.

The last objective is to gain microscopic and dynamic views of cross-native/community language families, especially in regard to families' decisions on their language use. While the data derived from the questionnaire survey reveal the present language situation of the families, they tell us little about why and how they have reached decisions on their language use. Nor do they tell us much about whether there have been any developmental changes in their language use over time. Follow-up interviews with a small subset of the subject families in the questionnaire survey are used for this final investigation.

Method

Subjects

The questionnaire was intended for families meeting the following three criteria:

Criterion 1: the family currently resides in Japan;
Criterion 2: the family consists of a parenting couple with at
least one child;
Criterion 3: the parents are from different native language
backgrounds.

With the cooperation of several individuals and organizations concerned with international families, 1,059 questionnaires were distributed, either by mail or in person, during the period from April to July 1996. Three hundred and ninety-seven questionnaires were returned (a response rate of 37.5%) but 37 of those were disqualified for failure to meet the three distribution criteria above, for reasons such as single-parenthood, childlessness, and so forth, leaving an adjusted response rate of 34.0% (360 remaining cases).

Criterion 4: The respondent completed all the questions
regarding familial language use
The main issue in the present study is to investigate and analyze language use among family members; for this purpose, complete information on who uses what languages to whom is indispensable. Of the 360 responses, 101 did not meet Criterion 4, leaving 259 responses.

Criterion 5: Each parent's native language is either Japanese
or English
On a further review of the remaining families, it was found that they consisted of one major group, Japanese–English families, and many

different other-language groups, each with a very small number of families. It was judged to be more fruitful to focus on the one major group with a sizable number of subjects than to try to treat a variety of language groups of different sizes as one sample, indiscriminately. Of the 259 responses, 77 did not meet Criterion 5, leaving 182.

Criterion 6: The youngest child is three years of age or older
It is a difficult task to determine when bilingual-to-be children become aware that they are being exposed to two separate languages and become able to differentiate them. As noted in Döpke (1992b), there have been two opposing positions in this debate: the 'immediate differentiation' hypothesis, that children are able to differentiate two languages from a very early age, and the 'initial one system' hypothesis, that children are not able to differentiate until a later stage. Among the studies supporting the first position are De Houwer (1990), Döpke (1992b), Genesee (1989), Lindholm and Padilla (1978), Meisel (1989), and Pye (1986); some supporting the latter are Imedadze (1967), Leopold (1978), Vihman (1985, 1986), and Volterra and Taeschner (1978).

Lyon (1996), proposing an alternative 'sequential' model, hypothesizes that children start to acquire the second language after reaching an optimal level in the first. She asserts that this optimal level is reached sometime around 24–30 months after birth and that 'children of [age] three are likely to be aware of language as well as able to use language (or languages)' (Lyon, 1996: 163).

There is not much point in examining what languages children use when they themselves are unaware of the languages and unable to differentiate them. Regardless of which position to support in the debate, which is not an issue here, a more conservative position should be taken for the purpose of the present study. Therefore, this study is restricted to children at least three years old, whose bilingualism would not be challenged on grounds of age by either camp.

Of the 182 responses, 64 did not meet Criterion 6, leaving 118 (hereafter, N-118), which will be the sample group to be analyzed. Figure 4.1 depicts the results of the selection procedure.

Materials and procedures

The questionnaire was prepared in two versions, a Japanese-language one and an English-language one (Appendix A). The contents of the two versions are equivalent, consisting of a checklist of family members and 15 questions. Both were sent, together with a cover letter and a self-

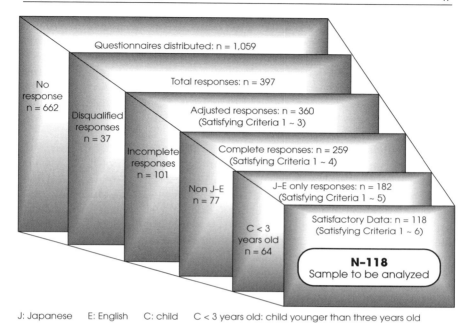

J: Japanese   E: English   C: child   C < 3 years old: child younger than three years old

Figure 4.1 Selection procedure for this study's data sample

addressed, stamped return envelope. The family was asked to fill out only the version of its preference but return both. Descriptions of and rationales for the questions are as follows.

Checklist of family members

The checklist was designed to have respondents confirm who their family members are and to prepare them for the questions.

Questions

The questions are grouped together into four main categories: (a) Family Background; (b) Family's Linguistic Situation; (c) Attitudes and Perceptions about Bilingualism; and (d) Promotion of Bilingualism.

(a) Family background

Family background questions request basic information, such as sex, age, nationality, and native language(s) of each member. The issue of what languages and how they are used among family members is a complicated matter, an interaction of various factors, such as the personal characteristics of the individual family members and even how many generations are living together in the same household. Data from one of the present author's previous surveys (Yamamoto, 1995) suggested, for example, that the presence of Japanese-speaking grandparents in the same household may affect patterns of language use in the family as a whole, especially between the parent who is a native speaker of non-Japanese and the children. It is therefore essential to collect these kinds of personal data on the family members.

The family's residential history since the birth of the first child was also asked. The same previous survey (Yamamoto,1995) did not find any significant relationship between success in bilingual child-rearing and the elements of family residential history, such as location, duration, and societal language(s) used. However, it does not seem unreasonable to assume that having some experience living in an area where a particular language is spoken may affect proficiency in that language and attitudes towards it, which may in turn affect the patterns of language use among family members and also parental attitudes towards bilingualism.

(b) Family's linguistic situation

Collecting information on the language use and linguistic environments of each family is the main purpose of this section. To obtain detailed data of language use among family members, respondents were asked to fill in a matrix form covering the languages used in communication between every possible pair of interlocutors, for example, the pJ and the first child, the pX and the first child, the first child and the second child, and so forth.

In addition to the macroscopic picture of language use in the family, a more microscopic investigation, that is how each individual actually uses languages, was attempted. The questionnaire asked the respondent whether and how frequently each member mixes languages in speaking to other family members.

Children spend their time not only in the family environment but also with their friends outside it. School-age children also spend much of their daily waking time at school. To grasp the children's overall linguistic environments, this section also included questions on the languages spoken by their friends and the language of formal instruction. The family's overall linguistic environments were probed in terms of opportunity that the family has for contact with non-Japanese speakers in the community.

It has been suggested that having a dream or a plan to return to the 'foreign' parent's native country may be an affecting factor for maintaining the language of that parent (Byram, 1990; Noguchi, 1999). Therefore, the questionnaire included a question on the family's plans to move to another area where languages other than Japanese are spoken.

(c) Attitudes and perceptions about bilingualism

The questions in this section were designed to identify some of the several possible factors encouraging or discouraging bilingualism. Lyon (1996) claims that parental attitudes along with local attitudes are likely to have a strong influence over language use in the family. It is not unreasonable to assume that if parents consider bilingualism to be detrimental, they will be discouraged from raising their children as bilingual. On the other hand, they may encourage bilingualism at home if they regard it as beneficial to their children.

Moreover, how the parents perceive the mainstream society's regard of bilingualism or of their own native languages may, in turn, affect their attitudes. It has been suggested that the esteem accorded to a minority language in the mainstream society is a factor affecting parental language use (e.g. Harding & Riley, 1986) or in the maintenance of that language (e.g. Paulston, 1994). The more prestigiously they perceive it to be viewed by the society, the more positive their own attitudes may be. The questionnaire therefore included items designed to uncover parental attitudes and perceptions.

Children who have negative feelings towards being raised in an interlingual family or who have had some undesirable experiences due to it may have quite different attitudes from those whose experiences have been more pleasant and positive. Since these attitudes may deeply affect children's bilingual development in terms of their language use, inquiries were also made into how the children themselves feel about their unique linguistic situations.

(d) Promotion of bilingualism

If parents try to raise their children bilingually, it is likely that they will establish a particular pattern of language use that exposes their children to both languages. To examine whether active promotion of bilingualism is reflected in the family's language use, the parents were asked whether they promote it or not.

Note

1. The questionnaire survey was supported by a Grant-in-Aid for Scientific Research (C), Project Number 07610517, funded by the Japanese Ministry of Education, Science and Culture.

Chapter 5
Findings

Data Description: Tabulation and Description

First, the linguistic milieu of the subject families is reported, based on data derived from the questionnaire survey. The data refer to family background, linguistic situations, attitudes and perceptions about bilingualism, and the parents' promoting efforts in bilingual child rearing.

Family background

The family background data of the subjects include the structure of the family, the family members' ages, nationalities, and native languages, and the family's experiences living in non-Japanese environments.

Family structure

Compared with the national statistics, the proportion of the three-generation families in the present sample is rather low. As of 1995, 23.0% (n = 4,594,000) of all the private households in Japan with a couple and offspring (n = 19,957,000) are three-generation families, with either one grandparent or both (*Kokuritsu Shakai Hoshou Jinkou-Mondai Kenkyuusho*, 1998).

By contrast, the majority of the subject families (n = 111 out of the total number of 118, 94.1%) are nuclear families, consisting of parents and their offspring (Figure 5.1; more detailed data are in Appendix B, Table B1). Only seven families (5.9%) in the whole sample are three-generation families. Of those seven, two families (1.7%) have two grandparents living with them, four (3.4%) have only a grandmother, and one (0.8%) has only a grandfather. None of the 118 families in the sample have other persons living in the same household.

Two explanations for this small proportion of three-generation families among the subjects may be suggested, one probabilistic and the other

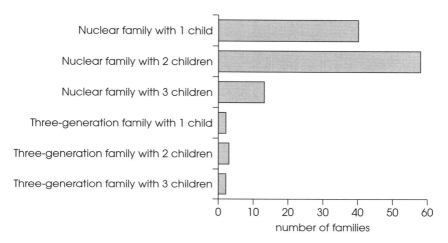

Figure 5.1 Family structures

cultural. Parents of the foreign spouse are more likely to be living outside of Japan. Thus, compared to most Japanese families, more of these cross-native/community language families are likely to have only one pair of grandparents (i.e. the Japanese pair) to accommodate, possibly living together under the same roof.

The cultural explanation reflects the fact that the majority of the foreign spouses in the present study are of American background (detailed data below in Nationalities of family members and Figure 5.5). According to a three-nation comparative survey of Japan, the United States of America, and South Korea (*Soumu-chou Seishounen Taisaku Honbu*, 1996), 63.5% of the Japanese subjects have a nuclear family, i.e. a family consisting of only a couple and their offspring, and 35.2% have a three-generation family, i.e. a family consisting of a couple, their offspring, and at least one grandparent. On the other hand, 93.9% of the American subjects have a nuclear family, and those who have a three-generation family amount only to 6.1%. The proportion of three-generation families in the present study may, therefore, exemplify the realities of internationally married couples living in Japan and reflect a certain compromise of two different cultures.

The number of children ranges from one to three, with large proportions of one-child (n = 42, 35.6%) or two-child (n = 61, 51.7%) families. Of this sample, only 15 families (12.7%) have three children.

Ages of family members

As shown in Figure 5.2 (more detailed data are in Appendix B, Table B2), most parents are in their 30s and 40s. Approximately half of the mothers (n = 56 out of the total number of 118, 47.5%) are in their 30s, with the youngest being 26 years old and the oldest being 54 years old. Slightly more than half of the fathers (n = 64 out of the total number of 118, 54.2%) are in their 40s, with the youngest being 28 and the oldest being 59.

The children's ages range from 3 to 28 (Figure 5.3; more detailed data are in Appendix B, Table B3). Most of the children are of either preschool age (ages: 3–6, n = 85 out of the total number of 209, 40.7%) or elementary school age (ages: 7–12; n = 89, 42.6%). Some are of junior high school age (ages: 13–15; n = 20, 9.6%) or senior high school age (ages: 16–18; n = 9, 4.3%), but very few are older (ages: 19–28; n = 6, 2.9%).

The ages of the grandmothers range from 65 to 77 and those of the grandfathers from 67 to 82 (Figure 5.4; more detailed data are in Appendix B, Table B4).

Nationalities of family members

All the adult family members have a single nationality, except one father, who is a dual national of the UK and Australia. Most of the parents hold either Japanese or American nationality: 49 mothers out of the total number of 118 (41.5%) with Japanese nationality and 58 (49.2%)

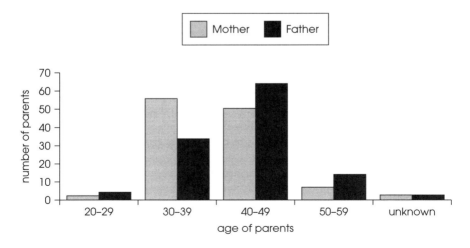

Figure 5.2 Ages of parents

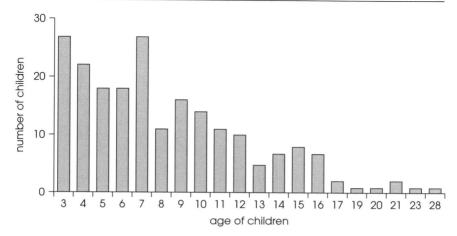

Figure 5.3 Ages of children

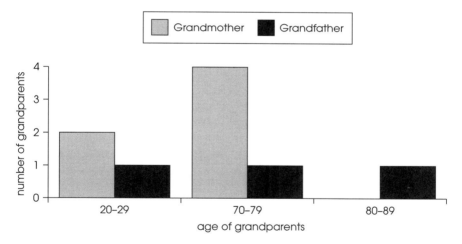

Figure 5.4 Ages of grandparents

with American nationality; and 68 fathers out of the total number of 118 (57.6%) with Japanese nationality and 39 (33.1%) with American nationality. The other countries represented in the data are Canada (mother: n = 1, 0.8%; father: n = 2, 1.7%), the UK (mother: n = 6, 5.1%; father: n = 8, 6.8%), Ireland (mother: n = 1, 0.8%), Australia (mother: n = 2, 1.7%), and New Zealand (mother: n = 1, 0.8%). All the grandparents have Japanese nationality (grandmother: n = 6; grandfather: n = 3).

In contrast, most of the children (n = 190 out of the total number of 209, 90.9%) hold dual nationalities: 109 out of the total number of 118 first children (C1) (92.4%), 68 out of the total number of 78 second children (C2) (89.5%), and 13 out of the total number of 15 third children (C3) (86.7%). Reflecting the variety of their parents' nationalities, the most frequently appearing combination of children's nationalities in this survey was Japanese–American nationality (n = 157, 75.1%), followed by that of Japanese–British (n = 19, 9.1%). There are two children (1.0%) with triple nationality of Japanese–American–Canadian. (See Figure 5.5; more detailed data are in Appendix B, Table B5.)

Until 1984, the Nationality Law permitted only Japanese fathers to pass on Japanese nationality to their children. Under this gender-based restriction, only children with Japanese fathers were able to hold multiple nationalities with Japanese and other nationalities, whereas those with Japanese mothers were excluded from this birthright. When the law was amended in 1984 and took effect in 1985, Japanese mothers also became entitled to pass their Japanese nationality on to their offspring. Since then, the number of multiple nationality holders has increased.

In principle, however, the law requires[1] multiple-nationality holders to renounce one of them when they reach the age of majority. Due to this requirement, the number of the multiple-nationality holders in the sample is subject to change.

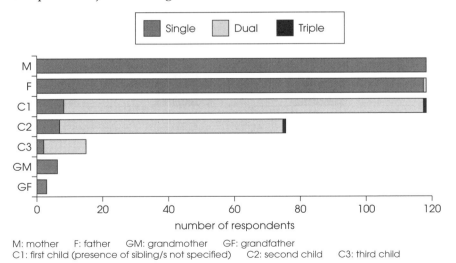

M: mother   F: father   GM: grandmother   GF: grandfather
C1: first child (presence of sibling/s not specified)   C2: second child   C3: third child

Figure 5.5 Nationalities of parents, grandparents, and children

Native languages of family members

Slightly more than half of the fathers (n = 68 out of the total number of 118, 57.6%) and somewhat less than half of the mothers (n = 50 out of the total number of 118, 42.4%) speak Japanese as their single native language. The numbers are reversed for those speaking English as their single native language. That is, 50 (42.4%) pairs of parents are a mother with Japanese and a father with English as their single native language, and 68 (57.6%) are a father with Japanese and a mother with English as their single native language (Figure 5.6; more detailed data are in Appendix B, Table B6). All of the grandparents are native speakers of Japanese.

Of all the children (n = 209), almost two-thirds (n = 126, 60.3%) are judged to be native speakers of both Japanese and English. The remaining 80 (38.3%) are judged to be native speakers of only one language, with 70 (33.5%) being judged as native speakers of Japanese and 10 (4.8%) being judged as native speakers of English. By birth order (i.e. C1, C2, and C3), approximately two-thirds of C1s (n = 75 out of the total number of 118), slightly less than two thirds of C2s (n = 45 out of the total number of 78), and less than half of C3s (n = 6 out of the total number of 15) are reported to be native Japanese–English bilinguals (hereafter, referred to as J–E bilinguals). None of C3s is judged to be a native speaker of English (Figure 5.7; more detailed data are in Appendix B, Table B7).

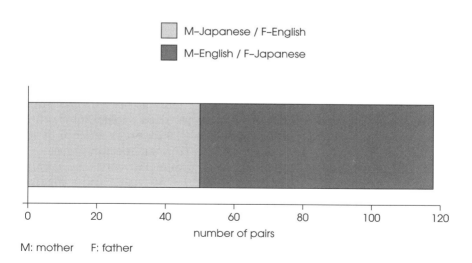

M–Japanese / F–English

M–English / F–Japanese

number of pairs

M: mother   F: father

Figure 5.6 Native languages of parents

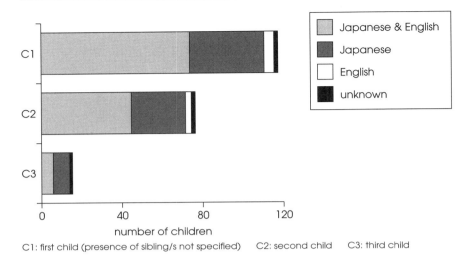

Figure 5.7 Native languages of children

Although all the children may eventually acquire bilingual fluency later in life, the data show clearly that not every child with parents of different native languages becomes spontaneously a native speaker of both.

Living experience in non-Japanese environments
Slightly more than a quarter of the families (n = 32 out of the total number of 118, 27.1%) have had experience living in non-Japanese environments for a year or longer since the first child was born, all but one of them in an English-speaking area (Figure 5.8; more detailed data are in Appendix B, Table 8). Four of these 32 families (12.5%) had additionally lived in areas where other languages were spoken (Singapore, Germany, China, and Nepal). The one family with no experience living in an English-speaking area had lived in a German-speaking area.
The length of stay in non-Japanese environments varies by family, ranging from one to 13 years, with a mean of 3.7 years, and a median of two years.

Family's linguistic situation

The family's linguistic situation includes what languages are used among the family members, how frequently each member switches

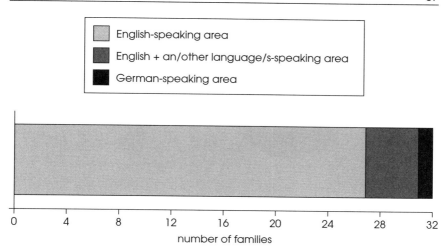

Figure 5.8 Family experience living in non-Japanese environments

languages, what opportunities there are for the children to be exposed to languages other than Japanese outside of the family, and whether or not the family plans to move to a non-Japanese-speaking area in the foreseeable future.

Languages used by pJs, pEs, and Cs

This section reports what languages are used by parents who are native speakers of Japanese (i.e. pJs), parents who are native speakers of English (i.e. pEs), and the children (i.e. Cs) in speaking to other members of the family (Figure 5.9; more detailed data are in Appendix B, Tables 9 and 10). A more detailed examination of language use, with a typological model of language use and a comparison of the present findings with those found in previous studies, is given below in Research Questions.

Regarding language interaction involving children, each child is separately considered. Thus, for parent–child language interaction, although there are only 118 pairs of parents, with 209 children we have 209 pairs of pJ and C (i.e. a parent who is a native speaker of Japanese and a child) and also 209 pairs of pE and C (i.e. a parent who is a native speaker of English and a child). For each pair, language interaction is counted separately from each interlocutor's point of view. Thus, we have 418 cases of pJ–C language interaction and likewise 418 cases of pE–C language interaction.

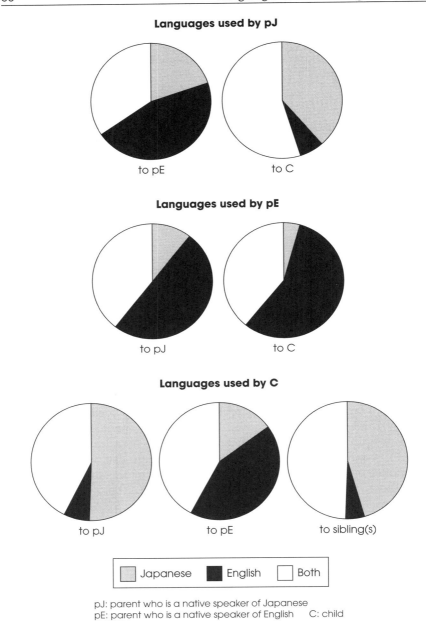

Figure 5.9 Languages used by pJs, pEs, and Cs

Up to this point, the designation C1 has been used to refer to both first-child subjects and only-child subjects. To analyze sibling interactions, however, it is necessary to distinguish them, hereafter using the designations C1-sib and C1-oc respectively. C2 and C3 refer to the second and third children, respectively.

There are 106 possible pairs of siblings among 167 children with sibling/s: 76 pairs of C1-sib and C2, 15 pairs of C2 and C3, and 15 pairs of C1-sib and C3. For every pair, language interaction is counted separately from each child's point of view. Thus, we have 212 cases of sibling language interaction in total: 76 cases of C1-sib addressing C2; 15 cases of C1-sib addressing C3; 76 cases of C2 addressing C1-sib; 15 cases of C2 addressing C3; 15 cases of C3 addressing C1-sib; and 15 cases of C3 addressing C2 (see Table 5.1). Needless to say, C1-oc subjects have no such interactive possibilities.

Table 5.1 Language interaction involving children

	Speaker	Addressed:	pJ	C1	C2	C3	Subtotal
pJ-C	pJ			118	76	15	209
language	C1		118				118
interaction	C2		76				76
	C3		15				15
				Total interaction cases: 418			

	Speaker	Addressed:	pE	C1	C2	C3	Subtotal
pE-C	pE			118	76	15	209
language	C1		118				118
interaction	C2		76				76
	C3		15				15
				Total interaction cases: 418			

	Speaker	Addressed:	C1-sib	C2	C3	Subtotal
sibling	C1-sib			76	15	91
language	C2		76		15	91
interaction	C3		15	15		30
			Total interaction cases: 212			

pJ: parent who is a native speaker of Japanese   pE: parent who is a native speaker of English   C: child   C1: first child (presence of sibling/s not specified)   C2: second child   C3: third child   C1-sib: first child, with sibling/s

(a) pJ ➡ pE

When speaking to their spouses, 78 out of the total number of 118 pJs (66.1%) use only one language, and in that case more pJs choose English (n = 54, 45.8%) than Japanese (n = 24, 20.3%). Approximately one-third of the pJs (n = 40, 33.9%) speak bilingually. None of the pJs use languages other than Japanese or English.

(b) pE ➡ pJ

Slightly fewer pEs (n = 72 out of the total number of 118, 61.0%) than pJs (n = 78, 66.1%) use one language in communicating with their partners. English (n = 60, 50.8%) is chosen by far more pEs than Japanese is (n = 12, 10.2%), similarly to the case of pJs speaking to pEs. Also, slightly more than one-third (n = 46, 39.0%) of the pEs speak bilingually. None of the pEs use languages other than Japanese or English.

(c) pJ ➡ C

Whereas monolingual communication is more frequent between spouses, as described above, more pJs seem to prefer to communicate bilingually with their children (n = 115 out of the total number of 209, 55.0%). In cases where only one language is used, Japanese is chosen by many more pJs (n = 82, 39.2%) than English is (n = 12, 5.7%).

(d) C ➡ pJ

In contrast to the pJs, there are more children who use only one language (n = 120 out of the total number of 209, 57.4%) than those who speak in both (n = 89, 42.6%). Children also overwhelmingly tend to choose Japanese (n = 106, 50.7%) rather than English (n = 14, 6.7%). It is interesting to note that in pJ–C interactions more children are inclined to use Japanese than their pJs are.

(e) pE ➡ C

While more pJs tend to use both languages in speaking to their children, more pEs prefer single language use (n = 128 out of the total number of 209, 61.2%). English is far preferred (n = 119, 56.9%) to Japanese (n = 9, 4.3%).

(f) C ➡ pE

More children speak monolingually (n = 121 out of the total number of 209, 57.9%) than bilingually (n = 88, 42.1%) in communication with their pEs. Although not as many as their pEs, more children also prefer English (n = 89, 42.6%) to Japanese (n = 32, 15.3%) in speaking to them.

It should be noted that while more pEs use English (n = 119, 56.9%) in speaking to their children than pJs use Japanese (n = 82, 39.2%), there are more cases in which children use Japanese to their pE (n = 32, 15.3%) than those in which they use English to their pJ (n = 14, 6.7%).

(g) C ➡ C

In communicating with a sibling, children are divided almost equally between those who use only one language and those who use both languages (n = 108 out of the total number of 212, 50.9%; n = 104, 49.1%). In the single-language-use group, Japanese (n = 98, 46.2%) is used by more children than English is (n = 10, 4.7%) (Appendix B, Table B10).

Code-mixing

Switching languages within the same utterance is common among bilingual speakers (Grosjean, 1982; Milroy & Muysken, 1995). Harding and Riley (1986: 119) state that 'code-switching comes naturally to a child brought up by people addressing him in two different languages.'

Under the umbrella term *code-switching*, one type of switching which occurs in the middle of a sentence, *intra-sentential* switching, is often referred to as *code-mixing* (Appel & Muysken, 1987). The questionnaire asked the subject families whether each member changes languages within a sentence, i.e. code-mixes, when speaking to each other. Their responses indicated that code-mixing is not unusual among the members of the subject families (Figure 5.10; more detailed data are in Appendix B, Table B11).

There are far more family members who code-mix to certain degrees than those who do not. Approximately one fifth of the family members (n = 94 out of the total number of 454, 20.7%) are reported to mix codes often. Slightly less than half (n = 213, 46.9%) reportedly do so sometimes. Somewhat under one-third (n = 128, 28.2%) are reported never to mix codes.

Opportunities to play with children from different language groups

Almost all the children have playmates who speak only Japanese (n = 203 out of the total number of 209, 97.1%), and many children often or sometimes play with friends who speak both Japanese and an/other language/s (n = 137, 65.6%) (Figure 5.11; more detailed data are in Appendix B, Table B12). However, only 75 (35.9%) of the children have some degree of chance to play with children who speak only a language other than Japanese.

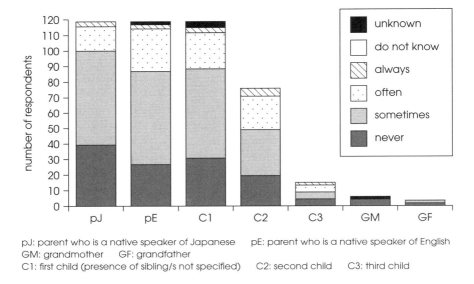

pJ: parent who is a native speaker of Japanese   pE: parent who is a native speaker of English
GM: grandmother   GF: grandfather
C1: first child (presence of sibling/s not specified)   C2: second child   C3: third child

Figure 5.10 Use of code-mixing

Language at school

Including kindergarten and preschool, most of the children (n = 197 out of the total number of 209, 94.3%) in the sample families attend some kind of school (Figure 5.12; more detailed data are in Appendix B, Table B13).

Of all 197 children in school, 60 children (30.5%) attend either preschool or kindergarten, 92 children (46.7%) attend elementary school, 22 children (11.2%) attend junior high school, and 15 (7.6%) children attend senior high school. Only four (2.0%) are in college/university and four more (2.0%) attend some other kind of school (Figure 5.13; more detailed data are in Appendix B, Table B14).

Regarding the type of school, the majority of the school-age children attend a Japanese school, either public or private (n = 157, 79.7%), and only 20 (10.2%) study at international schools. Six (3.0%) attend some other type of school (Figure 5.14; more detailed data are in Appendix B, Table B15).

For an overwhelming number of cases (n = 165, 83.8%), the medium of instruction at school is Japanese. Twenty-five children (12.7%) receive instruction in English only, while six children (3.0%) receive instruction bilingually, with five of them in Japanese and English (2.5%) and one in Japanese and Korean (0.5%). The ratio of school language seems to

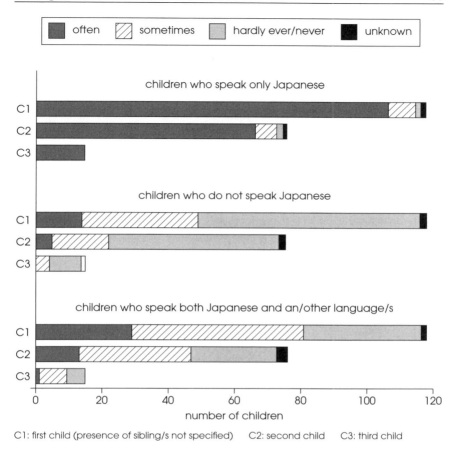

Figure 5.11 Play opportunities, sorted by playmate language group

reflect that of school type, i.e. Japanese language in Japanese school and English in international school (Figure 5.15; more detailed data are in Appendix B, Table B16).

The data show that most children are not enrolled in an international school (n = 163, 82.7%), nor are they receiving any formal instruction in English (n = 166, 84.3%).

This low enrollment rate in international school/English-medium schools may be explained, on the one hand, by the poor accessibility of such schools in regard to number, location, and expense. As of 1994, there were only 27 English-medium international schools which are

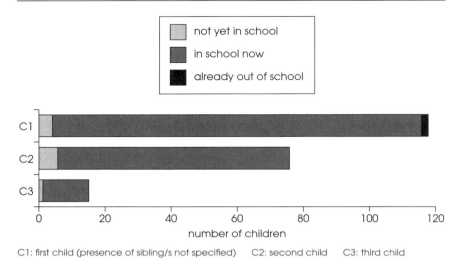

Figure 5.12 School enrollment

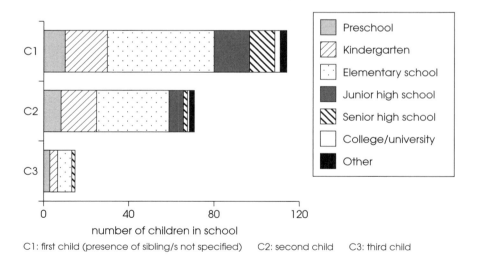

Figure 5.13 Level of school

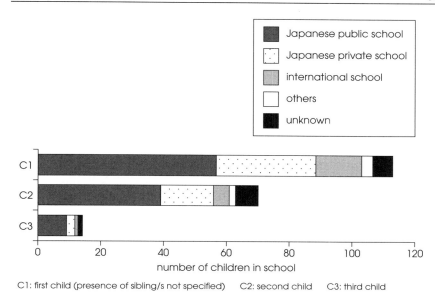

Figure 5.14 Type of school

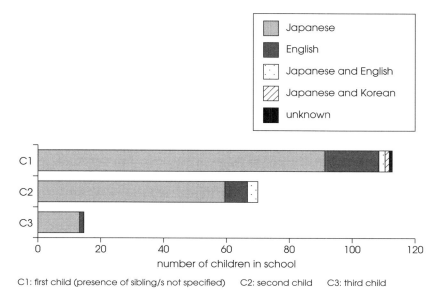

Figure 5.15 Medium of instruction

members of the Japan Council of International Schools (Japan Council of International Schools/Ministry of Education, Science, Sports and Culture, 1994). The schools are generally small; the student capacity of the schools vary from the smallest of 150 to the largest of 1,454. Some schools have classes at all levels, from kindergarten through high school, while others offer classes only at some levels.

In addition to the limited numbers of international schools, access to them is also limited mainly to the major cities: twelve are located in Tokyo, three each are in Yokohama and Kobe, with one each in Sapporo, Sendai, Nagoya, Nara, Osaka, Kyoto, Hiroshima, Fukuoka, and Okinawa. Thus, they are physically accessible only to those who live within reasonable commuting distance of such cities.

High tuition fees also make international schools less accessible. Annual tuitions range from approximately ¥1,000,000–2,000,000 (approx. US$9,000–18,000) or even more. In contrast, school-related expenses for Japanese public schools are much lower. According to a survey (Ministry of Education, Science, Sports and Culture, 1997), the educational expenses during the 1994 school year were, on average, a little less than ¥100,000 (approx. US$900) (school lunch included) at the elementary level, slightly less than ¥170,000 (approx. US$1,500) (school lunch included) at the junior high school level, and a little over ¥310,000 (approx. US$2,800) (no school lunch included) at the senior high school level. Even to those who sent their children to private (Japanese-medium) schools, related expenses were not as high as a million yen.

Beyond matters of accessibility, the status of international schools in the Japanese school system may also make parents hesitate to choose an international school over a Japanese school. The majority of these English-medium international schools, 20 out of the 27, are authorized as 'miscellaneous schools' by the Prefectural Governments in their district. Such schools are not given regular Japanese school status, but are defined only as 'institutions similar to' regular schools. The remaining seven schools are not even registered as miscellaneous schools. The disadvantageous official status of international schools may hinder international school graduates from advancing through the Japanese school system, especially at the level beyond compulsory education.

On the other hand, the low enrollment may well be a result of an active family choice of a Japanese school over an international school. According to Moon (1991), in a questionnaire survey to a group of foreign mothers married to Japanese men, under the condition that both location and finances would permit any choice, more mothers favor Japanese schools over international schools for their children's education from

preschool/kindergarten through high school: preschool/kindergarten
(Japanese school–76%, International school–6%, Other–18%, Undecided–
0%); elementary school (88%, 8%, 4%, 0%, respectively); junior high
school (72%, 18%, 8%, 2%, respectively); high school (46%, 24%, 16%,
6%, respectively and 'let their children decide' – 8%).

Location of residence
The most common area of residence is a residential area in a suburb,
which accounts for slightly less than half of the families (n = 57 out of
the total number of 118, 48.3%). No family in this survey lives in a factory
area (Figure 5.16; more detailed data are in Appendix B, Table B17).

Opportunities for meeting non-Japanese speakers
The families are fairly evenly divided between those who have 'some'
or 'many' opportunities to meet speakers of languages other than
Japanese (n = 64 out of the total number of 118, 54.2%) and those who
have 'none' or 'few' opportunities (n = 52, 44.1%) (Figure 5.17; more
detailed data are in Appendix B, Table B18).

Plan to move to non-Japanese-speaking areas
The majority of the families (n = 101 out of the total number of 118,
85.6%) have no specific plan in the near future to move to an area where
languages other than Japanese are spoken. Of those who do (n = 13,

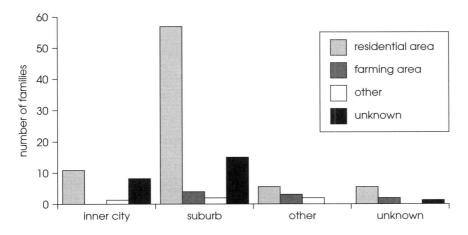

Figure 5.16 Location of residence

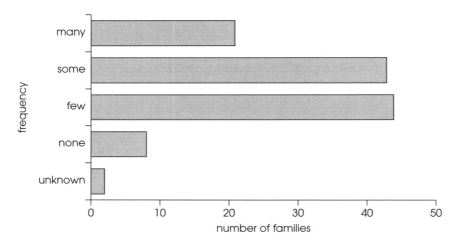

Figure 5.17 Opportunities for meeting non-Japanese speakers

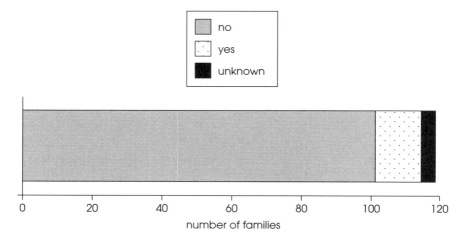

Figure 5.18 Plan to move to non-Japanese-speaking areas

11.0%) all intend to move to an English-speaking area (Figure 5.18; more detailed data are in Appendix B, Table B19).

Attitudes and perceptions about bilingualism

Parental attitudes towards bilingualism
Most of the parents have positive attitudes towards bilingualism (Figure 5.19; more detailed data are in Appendix B, Table B20). Of the total number of 118 families, 104 families (88.1%) think that being bilingual is beneficial. Although none considers bilingualism to be purely detrimental, some (n = 12, 10.2%) express ambivalent feelings, claiming it to be both beneficial and detrimental. It is worth noting that this ratio closely duplicates the ratio obtained in the 1990 survey by the present author: beneficial = 87.8%, detrimental = 0%, both = 10.2% (Yamamoto, 1995).

The reasons given by those who emphasize the benefits of being bilingual center around five major aspects: practicality, interpersonal communication, cross-cultural understanding, character-building, and cognitive development.

From the viewpoint of practicality, many parents think that being bilingual is advantageous in the job market as well as for academic advancement, and that it provides more opportunities and options. It is thought to be useful as a skill. Parents also feel that being able to speak more than one language comes in handy when traveling. Bilingual abilities allow their children to go to school or live abroad, and ensure that they will not be confined only to Japan. Bilingualism is believed to increase one's choices and opportunities in general. An American mother

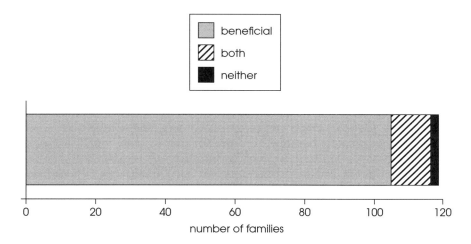

Figure 5.19 Attitudes towards bilingualism

(ID#219), age 41, with an eight-year-old boy and a five-year-old girl,[2] even thinks that '[i]n the long run, being bilingual or multilingual is financially beneficial.'

Some parents also consider being bilingual rather beneficial from the standpoint of interpersonal communication. One of the major concerns that parents have is to develop good communication with their two sets of extended families as well as within the family. Having bilingual ability enables them to do so. Parents also believe that it helps the children communicate with a wider variety of people in the world.

Bilingualism is also thought to be beneficial in terms of cross-cultural understanding. It is believed to help the children understand not only the cultures of both parents, but also other cultures as well. As a consequence, one can broaden her/his outlook and respect other ways of thinking.

Some think that being bilingual enhances one's open-mindedness. It helps people to develop flexibility and tolerance towards a variety of values and also helps them to look at themselves objectively.

Bilingualism is helpful not only for character-building but also for cognitive development. Some parents claim that analytical thinking and intellectual advancement can be expected.

Other miscellaneous reasons put forward were that being bilingual is simply fun and that greater knowledge is a good thing.

Those who feel that bilingualism has negative aspects, although admitting that it also has its positive side, explain their position in terms of language deficiency, social stigma, and conflicting identities. Some parents believe that their children's vocabulary is limited compared with other children. A British mother [ID#158–48: boy-16/girl-9] even claims that language deficiency causes her family some difficulty in 'in-depth discussions':

> It is useful and enjoyable to be able to communicate in more than one language. However, during their younger years children may be less adept in either language than their peers. In our case our son in particular, because he does not like to read much, is rather limited in vocabulary we feel. In addition, as we are, as a family, all at different levels of competence in our 2 languages, it is difficult for us to have really in-depth discussions.

Being viewed as different also affects some families negatively. Their children are made to feel outcast or strange by their peers. Some parents feel that dealing with dual linguistic, cultural, social, or educational systems causes their children some confusion and anxiety. A Japanese mother [ID#253–40: boy–16/boy–5] who married a Briton points out that 'in the Japanese society bilinguals still tend to be thought of as having dual personalities, and due to that, I feel they are sometimes not accepted as members of the society' [present author's translation].

General Japanese perception of bilinguals
Almost all the respondents feel that in general, ordinary Japanese people perceive J-E bilinguals positively: 'very positively' (n = 78 out of the total number of 118, 66.1%) or 'somewhat positively' (n = 33, 28.0%) (Figure 5.20; more detailed data are in Appendix B, Table B21).

However, quite a number of the respondents express a different view when it comes to bilingualism in other languages (Figure 5.21; more detailed data are in Appendix B, Table B22). A little over two-thirds of those who answered the question (n = 75, 63.6%) believe that Japanese people in general perceive non-J–E bilinguals differently from J–E bilinguals. Since almost all the parents think that J–E bilinguals are perceived positively, this response implies that they think that non-J–E bilinguals are taken less positively. Only slightly under a third (n = 33, 28.0%) feel that the particular combination of languages does not make any difference.

Those who think that non-J–E bilinguals are perceived differently from J–E ones view English as being placed on a higher, if not the highest,

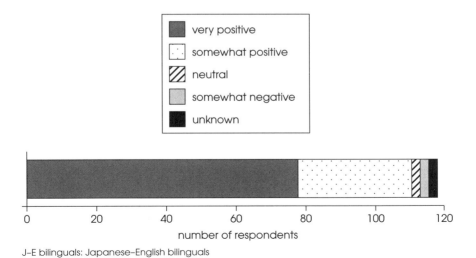

J–E bilinguals: Japanese–English bilinguals

Figure 5.20 Assessment of Japanese perception of J-E bilinguals

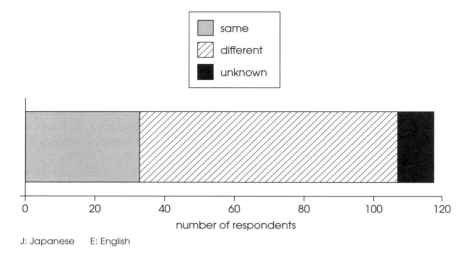

Figure 5.21 Assessment of Japanese perception of language combinations other than J-E

position in the 'status ladder,' and many of them give practical reasons for why this might be so. One such reason is that English is an 'international' language and, therefore, useful and valuable worldwide. Another reason is that it is one of the core subjects in entrance examinations in Japan; being good at it gives one academic advantages. Thus, J–E bilinguals are admired rather highly, whereas bilinguals of other less 'prestigious' languages are not admired as much.

Some point out a bias towards or against particular languages as a reason why they believe some difference in perception exists based on the languages bilinguals speak. They feel that languages are divided into two major groups: European languages, on the one hand, with English being most preferred, and non-European languages, such as the Asian and African languages, on the other. Languages in the former group, especially English, are putatively more highly esteemed than those in the latter group. A Japanese mother [ID#105–29: girl–3] who married an American states that '[many Japanese] are relatively favorable towards languages such as French and German, which can be mainly used in Europe and America' [present author's translation].

On the other hand, 'Asian languages, African languages tend to be generally thought of as "inferior"' (an American mother [ID#37–45: boy–13/boy–9]) and '[t]here is absolute discrimination among Japanese of Asian, African, Arab, or South American languages' (an American mother [ID#151–32: boy–5/girl–3]). An American mother [ID#219 above–41: boy–8/girl–5] plainly points out the Japanese 'blind belief' in English, stating that:

> There is a definite hierarchy of the way languages are perceived. English at the top – followed by common European languages. My Phillipina [sic] and Polish friends have gotten no positive support for speaking Tagalog or Polish with their kids – however, people do see their somewhat broken English as being worthwhile. A pity.

It seems that this discriminatory 'rank-order' given to different languages is also extended to their speakers. A British mother [ID#158 above–48: boy–16/ girl–9] states that 'I doubt if there is a positive attitude to Chinese, Korean, etc. speakers, or to speakers of languages from low-profile countries, e.g. African countries, South American countries, etc.' Another observation comes from an American father [ID#84–age–not given: boy–13/girl–11/girl–7], who asserts that 'Koreans and Chinese who speak excellent Japanese seem less admired than non-Asian speakers are.'

Linguistic issues often go hand in hand with racial issues. The issue here is assumed to be a linguistic one: whether combinations of languages of bilinguals affect how they are perceived or not. Many respondents, however, commented on racial issues hidden behind the difference in perception of bilinguals.

An American mother [ID#233–39: boy–7/boy–5/boy–3] describes the issue as '[t]he prejudice to want to be like a "white western person" vs another nationality/race.' An American father [ID#105 above–29: girl–3], also asserts clearly that the issue is a racial matter rather than a linguistic one: '[n]ative English speakers (especially white Westerners) do not generally experience as much racial discrimination as non-white foreigners.' Behind the prejudice in favor of white westerners, an American father [ID#80–44: girl–11/girl–9] points out that '[m]any Japanese have a superiority complex towards other Asians.' A Japanese mother [ID#316–45: girl–10/boy–8] who married an American also asserts that '(in Japan) there is a lot of prejudice against economically less powerful countries, those whose populations are considered by Japanese to be racially inferior, Asians, etc' [present author's translation].

The linguistic issues and racial issues are closely interlocked. An American mother [ID#19–37: boy–8/girl–5] states:

> I have friends from less 'high-status' countries (i.e. India, Switzerland) & they say that their acquaintances put down their efforts to

bring up their children bi-lingually (esp. in a lesser-known language in India). Japanese people must realize that 'internationalizm' [sic] is *not* equivalent to 'American' or 'English.' There are hundreds of languages in the world, all equally valid, yet to so many Japanese, the blond, blue-eyed people like me are the only 'GOOD' foreigners. How narrow-minded and ridiculous! I'm very lucky, yet I have less lucky friends.

The issue of bilingualism also touches upon the issue of Japanese ethnic purity. A Japanese father [ID#249–59: boy–28/girl–23/girl–16] who married an American comments:

On the surface, bilinguals are perceived positively, for practical reasons, such as that being bilingual is more advantageous in entrance examinations or on the job. However, I detect that people perceive being bilingual as a profanity against the pure Japanese atmosphere and hold strong feelings of both repulsion and jealousy. It resembles the way that people perceive mixed-blooded people. I think that people hold more negative perceptions towards bilingualism, especially in combinations involving non-European/ American languages such as Korean [present author's translation].

On the other hand, some who think no difference is detected refer to the sheer admiration of Japanese people towards bilingualism, irrespective of the particular languages involved. An American mother [ID#18–43: boy–12] asserts that '[s]ince most [Japanese] only speak 1 language they seem to respect anyone who can speak more than one.' Similar comments were also given by Japanese respondents.

Children's negative reactions to being addressed in English in the presence of their Japanese friends

Slightly more than one-third of the subject families (n = 44 out of the total number of 118, 37.3%) claim that they have encountered negative reactions from their children when they speak to them in English in the presence of their Japanese friends. The remaining families, except two with no answer, (n = 72, 61.0%) reported no negative experiences (Figure 5.22; more detailed data are in Appendix B, Table B23).

Some children are wholly resentful at being addressed publicly in English. One way that children cope with such a situation is to ignore the parent who is speaking to them in English. An American father [ID#84 above-age-not given: boy–13/girl–11/girl–7], referring to the reaction of his 11-year-old daughter, says 'if we're in public in Japan, she'll

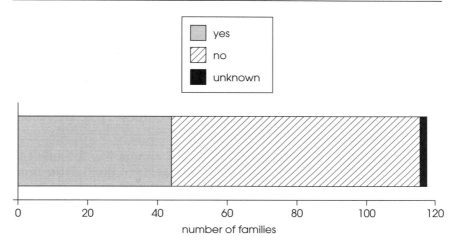

Figure 5.22 Children's negative reaction to being addressed in English

ignore me and try to make me be quiet or she'll walk away.' Other children, not reacting that extremely, ask their parents not to speak English in public. Similar reactions are also reported by some Japanese parents who tried to speak to their children in English. Most parents seem to be sympathetic to the feelings of their children, and try to either comply with their requests or compromise by lowering their voices while speaking in English.

Some parents, however, take rather different approaches. One of them is an American mother [ID#118–34: boy–9/girl–7] who discussed the issue with her children:

> My daughter was teased for being (looking) a foreigner in kindergarten and asked (her mother) me at that time not to speak to her in English in front of [her] kindergarten friends. We talked about what being foreign meant and how to deal with our feelings when someone said something hurtful. We also talked about the difference between someone stating a fact, that we are foreign, and someone trying to hurt our feelings. I also asked her teacher to be aware of the situation.

Yet another approach is taken by a Canadian mother [ID#209–38: girl–11/ boy–4]. She reports that '[w]e explained to her that in our home we speak two languages; if her friends don't like it, then it is their problem. She has changed friends [to some] that are more positive now.'

Some children so badly resent being spoken to in English in public that their family stops speaking it entirely. It seems, however, that a lot of children overcome this 'uncomfortable' feeling in time and actually start enjoying being able to use English, re-interpreting it as advantageous. Several families commented on the fact that their children reacted negatively when they were younger but stopped doing so after getting older. An American mother [ID#33–40: girl–10/boy–7] describes her experience:

> Both kids went through a phase between around 5 and 7 (the age at which their friends realized they were different through the transition into elementary school) when they wanted to downplay the fact that they were bilingual ('half'/different in general). Our daughter never seemed to be as bothered by this as our son, who experienced a short, strong 'blast' at 5–6. He was perfectly willing to speak [English] with me alone/at home – but specifically asked me not to use it when I picked him up at day care. Now they both think it's totally cool (although they sometimes respond to me in Japanese in the presence of their friends).

An American father [ID#2–45: girl–8] expresses his surprise at his daughter's drastic change within one year:

> At my daughter's elementary school this happened in her first year. I lowered my voice and continued to use English. I allowed *her* to use Japanese. But now she's in an English club there with other kids who speak English & she is now EAGER to speak English in front of her non-bilingual friends! (A very dramatic change.)

The attitudinal transition from being negative to positive, however, may be language-specific. In this, the advantageous position of English over other languages is further detected. An American mother [ID#19 above–37: boy–8/ girl–5] comments:

> In kindergarten [the older child] would take me aside and say, 'Don't talk to me in English. *Boku wa iyada-yo!* [I don't like it!: present author's translation]' In 1st grade he was even more sensitive in the new environment & a 3rd grade boy teased him & made him extremely upset. He couldn't see anything good about being bilingual & bi-cultural & *different*. In the past 2 years, though, he has realized that his friends think it's *chou-ii* [super cool: present author's translation] that he can speak English & he has gradually come to enjoy the attention he receives (he has always loved attention) & is

very proud now of his English ability. Since he is very conscious of his friends' opinions, I'm glad his second language is English, as no other foreign language is as admired in Japan. What I have always done on these occasions of negative reactions is stress the benefits of being bilingual and point out that ignorance or envy often causes kids to react to [the son's name deleted for privacy] in this way.

Another parent tries to understand her children's negative reactions from a more general viewpoint, as behavior typical of teenage boys. An American mother [ID#41–49: girl–21/boy–16] states:

13–15-year-old boys don't want their mothers to speak in public, period. When Japanese is used, they are afraid you'll give away some 'baby-like' information about them. When English is used, they are afraid you'll collect a swarm of girls around you. This is more about under-classman low profile than either language. For teenaged boys, moms aren't cool!

Many families who allegedly never experienced negative reactions from their children think that it is so because their children are still too young. Some of them foresee that it might happen later.

Other families take the 'precautionary measure' of not speaking English to their children in front of their friends, so that they will not be teased. An American father [ID#144–49: boy–11] states that 'I make it a policy to speak in Japanese in the presence of the child's Japanese friends.' Some children, on the contrary, react negatively when their pEs try to speak in Japanese. An American mother [ID#157–age–not given: boy–7] says that '[s]o far my son doesn't want me to speak *Japanese* – my Japanese isn't very good. He doesn't mind me speaking English anywhere – (yet).'

Because of the widely varying reactions, as described above, it is very difficult to generalize how children will react to their bilingual environment. However, why they react the way they do seems to be suggested in many comments. It is not their being addressed in English by their parents itself that makes them react the way they do, but how their peers react to it. Children react negatively if their peers react negatively by teasing or ostracizing them for being different or being bilingual. Thus, if their friends view their being bilingual as something advantageous and enviable, they are likely to react positively, as reported in the comments above.

Children also try to avoid attracting public attention. Their parents speaking a language other than Japanese in public definitely distinguishes them from everyone else. They are making their very best effort to shunt the center of public attention away from themselves. A comment by a Japanese father [ID#249 above–59: boy–28/girl–23/girl–16] who married an American reveals children's rather complicated state of mind:

> [Our children] disliked being spoken to in English by their American mother during their kindergarten and elementary school ages. Especially, our son, the first child, did most. Because of it, the mother stopped speaking to him in English in the presence of his friends. Then, around the time when he started junior high school, he conversely wanted her to speak in English. It is because when she spoke Japanese to him in public, for example in a train, people nearby turned around to look at them [present author's translation].

Specific experiences due to the fact that they were born and raised in a cross-native/community language family

Slightly less than three quarters (n = 85 out of the total number of 118, 72.0%) of the respondents claim that their children have had some specific experiences – desirable and/or undesirable – due to the fact that they were born and raised in a cross-native/community language family. Of these 85 respondents, 21 (17.8%) report desirable experiences, 17 (14.4%) undesirable ones, and 47 (39.8%) both desirable and undesirable ones. Those who claim that they have had no such experiences are 32 (27.1%) (Figure 5.23; more detailed data are in Appendix B, Table B24).

Most of the desirable experiences reported refer to children being bilingual and bicultural. Many children are often complimented and envied by their friends, classmates, and adults around them for their bilingual abilities. With their bilingual and bicultural backgrounds, the children have beneficial experiences such as being able to make friends in both countries, 'meet and share experiences with people who they would otherwise not be able to communicate with' (an American mother [ID#118 above–34: boy–9/girl–7]), and 'have a wider variety of experiences than most of their friends' (an American mother [ID#175–43: girl–9/girl–6]). Some children reportedly enjoy academic advantages in their English classes and tests.

Among all the undesirable experiences, the most frequently mentioned one was being pointed at and called names, such as *gaijin* (foreigner), *gaijin-no-ko* (foreigner's kid), *haafu* (half-breed), and *eigo no hito* (English-speaking person). This is done for teasing in some cases and in other cases merely for stating the fact. Either way, it is perceived as unpleasant. The message they receive is clear: 'they are not accepted as Japanese

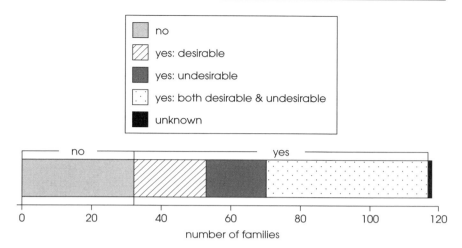

no

yes: desirable

yes: undesirable

yes: both desirable & undesirable

unknown

Figure 5.23 Specific experiences

because of the foreign blood introduced through their parent' (an American mother [ID#81–32: boy–4/girl–3]).

Related to this, several parents point out that unpleasant experiences they have encountered stem from 'biracial' or bicultural, rather than bilingual, features attributed to cross-native/community language families. An American father [ID#105 above–29: girl–3] says that:

> We have occasionally gotten dirty looks from strangers on the train, but as with question number 12 [*Do you think bilinguals speaking other combinations of languages are perceived the same way in Japan?*], this is more likely because we are a *biracial* family rather than because we are a bilingual family.

An American mother [ID#37 above–45: boy–13/boy–9] also claims that:

> Bicultural more than bilingual – Being called a stupid American, stupid foreigner by classmates, simply because the classmates knew their mother was American. One classmate refusing to come over to play at our house because Americans all have guns and therefore he was afraid!

Another unpleasant experience often mentioned is that children are told to say something in English by other children. An American mother [ID#113–41: boy–15/girl–12] describes this humiliating experience like '[t]hey have to "perform" like pet monkeys.' It seems to be one form of bullying. Another American mother [ID#235–45: boy–13/boy–10] reports her son's experience:

> It is not pleasant for a preschooler (our oldest) to be surrounded by 8–10 elementary school kids who are all saying *'eigo de nanika ieyou* [Say something in English: present author's translation].'

Repeatedly having such experiences can cause a child to act as if he did not speak English, but only Japanese, in an effort to avoid another undesirable experience. An American mother [ID#19 above–37: boy–8/ girl–5] writes:

> When he was young, my 8-yr. old would go to the park with me and other kids would say *'GAIJIN!'* [foreigner: present author's translation] or *'Gaijin no ko!'* [foreigner's kid: present author's translation] and he *hated* it. So we tended to avoid crowded parks. Even in our neighborhood, he hated to be noticed because of me or asked to speak English. If he heard the word GAIJIN, he'd talk to me loudly in Japanese. It was a lot of stress. At kindergarten, he took a month off in December when we visited the U.S. When he came back, some kids would say *'Eigo shabere-yo!'* [Speak English: present author's translation] & he came home in tears and asked me, 'Mommy, why is it only me who speaks English?'

In regard to speaking English, children are not the only ones who bring bilingual children unpleasant experiences. An American mother [ID#41 above–49: girl–21/boy–16] reported her children's undesirable experiences with their English teachers at school:

> Near beligerence [sic], certainly over sensitive egos of *middle aged male English teachers* in high schools. Some have made it abundantly clear (in both children's cases) that they were not happy the children were there and that the teachers were uncomfortable. Not a pleasant experience for either child.

Grandparents are no exceptions. An American mother [ID#71–37: boy–6/girl–3] states that 'Japanese grandparents have reprimanded the kids for using [English] within earshot or in their house (we visit weekly at a minimum, sometimes daily) – they are harsh in their reprimands.'

An American father whose children had no unpleasant experiences [ID#38–40: girl–7/boy–3] thinks that it is due to the fact that the children's Japanese is as good as that of their peers and the family has been living in the same neighborhood for a long time.

Promotion of bilingualism

The majority of the families (n = 106 out of the total number of 118, 89.8%) claim that they are trying to raise their children to be bilingual. Only six (5.1%) say that they are not (Figure 5.24; more detailed data are in Appendix B, Table B25).

In answer to the question why they promote bilingualism in their child-rearing, many parents repeated or referred to the same reasons why they think bilingualism is beneficial (Q10): practicality, interpersonal communication, cross-cultural understanding, character-building, and cognitive development. Those who give reasons from the practical viewpoint believe that bilingualism gives their children more options for their future, such as choices in education, location to live, career, and even nationality. An American mother [ID#175 above–43: girl–9/girl–6] feels that it is parents' 'duty to make [the children] comfortable in both languages/cultures so if they have to choose a nationality it isn't by default, but a freely made choice.'

Many parents are trying to raise their children to be bilingual so that they can communicate with their relatives on both sides. An American father [ID#105 above–29: girl–3] says that 'she has relatives who can speak only English or Japanese. It would be a sad thing, for example, if she needed an interpreter to speak with her American grandmother.'

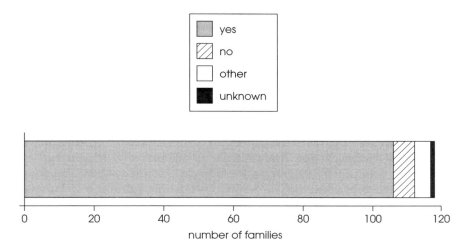

Figure 5.24 Promotion of bilingualism

Some parents express the same sentiment with the communication between their children and themselves, due to their lack of proficiency in Japanese. They feel it necessary to raise their children to be bilingual so that they can communicate well with their children. An American mother [ID#206–31: girl–7/boy–4] states that '[w]e feel there is no alternative. I speak only English well yet we live in Japan.' Even an American mother [ID#219 above–41: boy–8/girl–5] who has some ability in Japanese gives as one of her reasons her fear of losing the means of communication with her children: 'simply because I know my children's ability to speak Japanese will soon surpass mine. I would hate to think there will be a day when we can't communicate.'

Some parents presume biculturalism along with bilingualism. By raising their children bilingually, the parents hope that their children will develop a deep understanding of both of their cultures. Further, they hope that experiences with two cultures will help them appreciate other cultures and people, to enrich their world. For character-building, an English mother [ID#187–44: boy–15/girl–4] promotes bilingual child-rearing 'to give my children self esteem, pride in who they are.' Some parents referred to advantages in mental development, greater mental flexibility or brain development as the reasons for raising children bilingually. Other parents believe that it is only natural for each parent to raise their children in her/his own native language. A British father [ID#78–35: girl–6] simply says that 'neither of us wants to raise a child while speaking a foreign language.' An American mother [ID#49–45: boy–4] expresses her feelings as follows:

> The reasons are countless – part of it may be a biological drive for me to teach my child his mother tongue. I couldn't imagine my child not speaking my language. I am motivated to teach him beyond my consciousness even. Although consciously I employ every technique known to me. I want the best for my child – I feel deeply this is the best for him.

There is even a parent who thinks that being raised to be bilingual is his child's 'birthright' (an American father [ID#108–47: girl–7]).

While raising their children to be bilingual, many parents also want the children to be bicultural. Referring to his monocultural background, an American father [ID#156–46: boy–12/girl–9] thinks that being bicultural is exciting: '[It is] [b]ecause I'm from a small, monocultural town, and I think having 2 languages and 2 cultures that you are native of/in is just about the most exciting thing imaginable.' There are also parents who promote bilingual child-rearing, hoping to broaden their children's horizons, enrich their lives, and help them develop positive attitudes towards differences.

It is worth noting that several parents make special remarks on the values of being proficient in English due to its usefulness in international communication. A British mother [ID#120–38: girl–7/boy–5] asserts that '[b]eing able to speak another language, especially English, widens their possibilities for the future.' In this light, it should be interesting to find out how parents of other minority languages feel about their own languages.

Among the families who are not trying to raise their children to be bilingual, it seems that some reached their decision with conviction while others were compelled to do so. There are parents who just do not want to force their children to be bilingual. An Irish mother [ID#23–37: boy–4], while speaking to her son in English, does not 'want to "force" [her] son to be bilingual.' She says that '[i]f he becomes bilingual it will be a bonus.' An American father [ID#144 above–49: boy–11] also speaks in English to his son, but is not insistent about it. He places priority on what he says to his son over how he says it. He adopts either language, depending on whether his son understands him or not.

Other parents take a 'first things first' approach. An American mother [ID#155–46: boy–14/boy–12/girl–9] feels that Japanese language and culture should come to the prime position in her children's life because they are growing up in Japan. The same feeling is shared by a Japanese mother [ID#262–35: boy–11/girl–10] who married a Briton. She asserts that it should be important for children first to master their primary language and establish their baseline identity. She cannot accept bilingualism which lacks reading and writing proficiencies.

Others express their regret for failing in their bilingual child-rearing. A British mother [ID#158 above–48: boy–16/girl–9] states with regret that both she and her husband once tried, but '[u]nfortunately, as soon as they started school their English – speaking ability faded.' An American mother [ID#25–49: girl–16/girl–11/boy–10] feels that it is very difficult to raise bilingual children when she is the only English source around, and feels guilty for not having kept it up.

Judging from the answers to the question on reasons to promote bilingual child-rearing, it seems that, to most families, bilingual child-rearing means providing their children with English at home. Likewise, most of their answers to the question regarding ways to do it are how to supply English to their children and how to maintain their constant exposure to it.

One of the basic means that many families described was their conscious use of language at home. Some families set English as a family language and try to use it exclusively among the family members, with Japanese being learned outside of the home. Others adopt the 'one parent–one language' principle, with each parent speaking her/his native language to their children. An American mother [ID#19 above–37: boy–8/girl–5] is so determined that she speaks exclusively English to her son even '[I]gnoring my son's negativism/ambivalence towards English & continuing to speak it.' Many parents also report that they read to their children in English, often at their bedtime, especially when they were young.

Along with their speaking and listening proficiencies, many parents concern themselves with their children's literacy, especially in English, since most of them go to a Japanese school where they can develop their literacy in Japanese. Some parents give lessons on a fixed schedule at home to teach reading/writing in English to their own children, either alone or with other children of a similar background. Some even enroll their children in distance education courses to have a more structured study program, including not merely English but also other subjects such as math, social studies, and history. This is often done concurrently with enrolling their children in a Japanese school.

Many families adopt audio/visual aids to increase the amount and extent of their children's exposure to English: videos/movies, TV shows, and audio cassettes in English. A few families mentioned that they mainly let their children watch English videos and TV programs. As a new technological addition to these products, computer software such as educational software in English, joined the traditional reading English storybooks and playing games in English. Taking children to the home country of the pE was also frequently mentioned. Many families make regular trips to visit their relatives. Some families enroll their children in a local school or summer camp during their stay.

Another way mentioned to increase exposure to English is participating in English-speaking events or informal gatherings. Some parents send their children to an English-speaking Sunday school or to a Japanese primary school with an English club. Some invite English-speaking friends and guests to their home so that their children can join them. Parents may also encourage their children to play with English-speaking friends or other bicultural children; some do this in a more organized way, by forming a playgroup in English. The group meets at a regular time and place, and the children can play together. Communicating with English-speaking relatives is also listed as a way to provide children with good opportunities to use English. If the relatives are unable to understand Japanese, children will not have any other choice but to use English to them.

Some families also commented on ways to encourage their children to want to be bilingual: one family tries to teach the children about the parents' cultures and religious values; another talks about the families and traditions in both countries; one pE shows her children that she is proud of her foreignness and not ashamed of being different.

Summary

The subject families mainly consist of nuclear families with a couple and their offspring. Very few are three-generation families. This small proportion of three-generation families may be accounted for by the fact that, living in Japan, each subject family has only one possible pair of grandparents to consider, since the other pair is likely to live outside of Japan. Also, it may not be customary for foreign spouses to consider living with their parents-in-law.

The number of children ranges from one to three, with two-child families predominating. Very few families have three children.

Most parents are in their 30s and 40s. The children's ages range from 3 to 28, and most of them are either preschool-age or elementary school-age. The ages of the grandparents range from 65 to 82.

Except one, all the parents have a single nationality, most of them either Japanese or American. Other nations represented among the subject families are Canada, Britain, Ireland, Australia, and New Zealand. All the grandparents have Japanese nationality. In contrast to the adults, most children hold dual nationality, most of them Japan–USA; two children have triple nationality.

All the parents are native speakers of either Japanese or English. All the grandparents speak only Japanese as their native language. There are far more children who are judged to be native speakers of both Japanese and English than those of only one language, either Japanese or English.

Slightly more than a quarter of the families have had experience living in non-Japanese environments for a year or longer since the first child was born. All those families except one had lived in an English-speaking area. The length of stay in those English-speaking environments ranges from one to 13 years, with an average of 3.7 years, and a median of two years.

In regard to language use, monolingual language use is more likely between the parents than bilingual language use with English being far more likely used than Japanese. In speaking to the children, more pJs seem to prefer to use both languages. When only one language is used, Japanese is greatly preferred. In contrast to the pJs, more children use only one language, Japanese over English. It is interesting that in pJ-C interactions more children tend to use Japanese than their pJs do. It seems that more pEs prefer single language use in speaking to their children, with English greatly preferred over Japanese. More children also tend to speak monolingually to their pEs, with English being favored, although not by as great a margin.

In communicating with a sibling, the children are divided almost equally between those who use only one language and those who use both languages. In the former group, Japanese is much more preferred than English.

Switching languages within a sentence seems to be common when the family members speak to each other. Except for the grandparents, the subjects who are reported never to code-mix are far outnumbered by those who do, to at least some degree.

Almost all the children have playmates who speak only Japanese, but approximately two-thirds of the children often or sometimes play with bi-/multi-lingual friends in Japanese and an/other language/s. One-third of the children have some chances to play with children who do not speak Japanese.

Most children attend some kind of school. One-third of them go to either preschool or kindergarten and slightly fewer than half attend elementary school. Others attend junior high school, senior high school, or college/university. The majority of the children study at Japanese school and receive instruction only in Japanese. Not many go to an international school where the medium of instruction is English. The low enrollment rate in international school/English-medium school may be accounted for, on the one hand, by the family's active choice of a Japanese school over an international school, and, on the other hand, by the inaccessibility of such schools in regard to number, location, expense, and status in the Japanese school system.

The families are fairly evenly divided between those who have 'some' or 'many' opportunities to meet speakers of languages other than Japanese and those who have 'none' or 'few' opportunities.

The majority of the families have no foreseeable plan to move out of Japan. All of those who do have a plan intend to move to an English-speaking area.

Most parents have positive attitudes towards bilingualism. They regard being bilingual as beneficial, from the viewpoint of practicality, interpersonal communication, cross-cultural understanding, character-building, and cognitive development. Whereas none think it to be purely detrimental, some claim it to be both beneficial and detrimental.

Almost all the parents feel that Japanese people in general perceive Japanese–English bilinguals positively. Quite a number of them, however, think that the ordinary Japanese perceive bilinguals of languages other than Japanese and English differently from Japanese–English bilinguals. Slightly fewer than a third think that the particular combination of languages makes no difference.

Slightly more than a third of the families have encountered some negative reaction from their children when parents speak to them in English in the presence of the children's Japanese friends.

More children have had some specific experiences, desirable and/or undesirable, than those who have not, due to their cross-native/community language family background. Most of the desirable experiences are regarding their being bilingual and bicultural. The most frequently mentioned undesirable experience was being pointed at and called names, such as *'gaijin'* (foreigner).

The majority of the parents are trying to raise their children to be bilingual. Many parents give reasons for their efforts from the viewpoints of practicality, interpersonal communication, cross-cultural understanding, character-building, and cognitive development.

Research Questions

In an attempt to analyze the language use among the family members and to investigate the factors that influence the children's language use, two specific research questions were asked: (1) Who uses what languages to whom? and (2) Under what circumstances is a child likely to speak in the minority-status language to its native-speaking parent?

Research question (1): Who uses what languages to whom?

The language use in cross-native/community language families can be modeled according to the typology outlined in the next section. This typology will act as a basis for analyzing the subject families. A comparison will be made between the findings from this analysis and those in previous studies.

A typology of language use in cross-native/community language families

Even when only two parental native languages (X and Y) are involved, there are nine possible combinations of language use between any two particular interlocutors, INT-1 and INT-2: both interlocutors use the same language, either X or Y; each interlocutor uses a different language, X or Y; one of the interlocutors uses either X or Y whereas the other uses both X and Y; or both interlocutors use both X and Y (see Figure 5.25).

Based on these nine possible combinations, a typological model of language use between each two particular interlocutors is formed (Figure 5.26). In interactions categorized as Types 1 and 2, pairs of interlocutors speak one and the same language to each other. Representing the societal language with an X and the minority language with a Y, interlocutors in Type 1 speak the societal language and in Type 2 interlocutors speak the minority language. These types are labeled as *Total Monolingual Use*: Total Monolingual Use in the societal language for Type 1 and Total Monolingual Use in the minority language for Type 2.

Interlocutors in Types 3 and 4 communicate to each other in a different language. One of the pair speaks the majority language and the other speaks the minority language. These two types may be characterized as *Collective Bilingual Use*: although only one language is spoken by each interlocutor, two languages are actually spoken between the pair as a whole. Each member is receptive to the other's opposite-language production.

INT-1	X	Y	X	Y	X	X+Y	Y	X+Y	X+Y
INT-2	X	Y	Y	X	X+Y	X	X+Y	Y	X+Y

Figure 5.25 Nine possible combinations of language use with language X and language Y

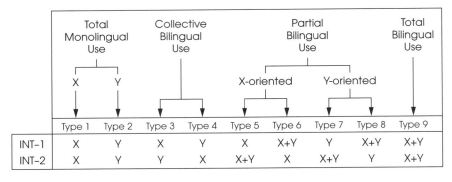

Figure 5.26 A typological model of language use between pairs of interlocutors

In interactions categorized as Types 5 to 8, one of the interlocutors speaks only one language whereas the other speaks two languages. In a majority language–minority language setting, the language spoken by the monolingual speaker in Types 5 and 6 is the majority language, and that spoken in Types 7 and 8 is the minority language. These four types may be termed *Partial Bilingual Use*, in which one of the interlocutors uses both languages actively, while the other is bilingual only passively. In contrast, in Type 9, termed *Total Bilingual Use*, both speakers adopt two languages productively in their communication with each other.

Types of language use in pairs of the subject families
Using this model, the language use between every possible pair of interlocutors in the subject families is categorized (Figure 5.27; more detailed data are in Appendix B, Table B26).

(a) Language use between pJ and pE
When we look at how the parents use languages with each other, it is found that Total Monolingual Use in English (Type 2: n = 54 out of

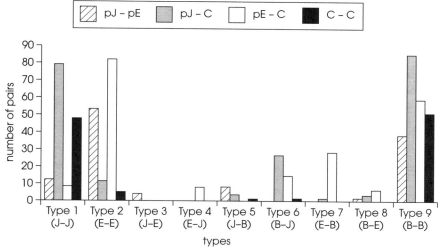

pJ: parent who is a native speaker of Japanese   pE: parent who is a native speaker of English
C: child   J: Japanese   E: English   B: both Japanese and English

Figure 5.27 Language use between every pair of interlocutors in the subject group

the total number of 118, 45.8%) is most commonly adopted, surpassing Total Monolingual Use in Japanese (Type 1: n = 12, 10.2%). This finding is in accord with those of Oka (1989), Shang (1997) and Yamamoto (1985, 1987, 1992, 1995), that the parents tend to choose one of their native languages as their common language, and that it is the non-Japanese language which is more likely to be chosen.

The fact that English is chosen more commonly than Japanese may be accounted for by differences in the parents' language abilities in each other's native language. Most pJs have received formal English classes at school for at least six years and acquired at least some knowledge of English through this exposure, even if they are not fluent. On the other hand, the same cannot be said about the pEs regarding their Japanese. In his survey report, McCarty (1999), for example, revealed that his Japanese subjects began studying English, on average, 27 years ago when they were 12 years old, whereas his English-speaking subjects started learning Japanese, on average, 16 years ago at the age of 25. The present author also found in the 1985 survey (Yamamoto, 1991) that more pEs (n = 38 out of the total number of 55) considered themselves to be monolingual in their native language than pJs (n = 27 out of the total number of 55) did. If these differences are also true of the present subjects, they may have influenced the parents' choice of English as their common language.

The next most commonly adopted pattern is Total Bilingual Use (Type 9: n = 38, 32.2%), in which both parents speak both Japanese and English to each other. The number of pairs who employ Partial Bilingual Use is very limited (Type 5: n = 8, 6.8% and Type 8: n = 2, 1.7%), and in all cases the parent who speaks monolingually uses her or his own native language. Only four couples (Type 3: n = 4, 3.4%) adopt Collective Bilingual Use, in which each partner speaks her or his own native language.

(b) Language use between pJ and children
Since Japanese is the native language of the pJ, it is most likely that Japanese would be the major means of communication between the pJ and children. The present data show, however, that Total Bilingual Use (Type 9: n = 85 out of the total number of 209, 40.7%) is more commonly adopted than Total Monolingual Use in Japanese (Type 1: n = 79, 37.8%), although the difference is small. This finding is not consistent with previous findings by Oka (1989) and Yamamoto (1985, 1987, 1992, 1995) in which Total Monolingual Use in Japanese was found to be most frequently employed. Very few pairs use English as a mutual means of communication (Type 2: n = 11, 5.3%).

It is interesting to note that whereas the pJ uses both languages, not a few children respond only in Japanese, Type 6 (n = 27, 12.9%).

(c) Language use between pE and children

In contrast to the language use between the pJ and the children, the native language of the pE, English, is the major vehicle of communication between the pE and children. Communication between them is most often in Total Monolingual Use in English (Type 2: n = 82 out of the total number of 209, 39.2%). This finding is consistent with previous findings by Oka (1989) and Yamamoto (1992, 1995). Total Bilingual Use is the next most common (Type 9: n = 59, 28.2%).

When the children are divided into two subgroups, 'only child' (C1-oc) and 'child with sibling/s' (C1-sib/C2/C3), some differences in their language use with the pE are observed: proportionately more only child-pE pairs communicate with each other in Total Monolingual Use in English (Type 2: n = 23 out of the total number of 42, 54.8%) than do child with sibling/s-pE pairs (n = 59 out of the total number of 167, 35.3%). On the other hand, in speaking with the pE, in absolute terms as well as proportionately, more children in the child with sibling/s group tend to use Japanese (n = 31, 18.6% [i.e. Type 1 (n = 9) + Type 4 (n = 7) + Type 6 (n = 15)]) than do those in the C1-oc group (n = 1, 2.4% [i.e. Type 4 (n = 1)]). The difference seems to suggest that the existence of siblings has some influence over the language use of the children. This observation is also evident in the children's choice of language for communicating with their sibling/s.

(d) Language use among siblings

Hoffmann (1985) has suggested that children are more exposed to the societal language through their siblings. Döpke (1992a) has pointed out that the majority language is usually used among siblings for communication. Findings from the present author's previous surveys (Yamamoto, 1985, 1987, 1992, 1995) provide corroborating evidence. In contrast, the present study found Total Monolingual Use in Japanese (Type 1: n = 48 out of the total number of 106, 45.3%) to be slightly less preferred among siblings; Total Bilingual use (Type 9: n = 51, 48.1%) was most preferred. Very few choose either Total Monolingual Use in English (Type 2: n = 5, 4.7%) or Japanese-oriented Partial Bilingual Use (Type 5: n = 1, 0.9% and Type 6: n = 1, 0.9%). No pair adopts Collective Bilingual Use (Type 3 and Type 4), nor English-oriented Partial Bilingual Use (Type 7 and Type 8).

Let us review the data from a slightly different perspective, that is, in terms of language concordance in parent–child pairs (i.e. how well the languages used by a parent and a child match). As seen above, a variety of language choice patterns is employed in the subject families, especially between the children and each of their parents. When the types used in parent–child pairs are carefully examined in terms of their language concordance, statistically significant differences are found between pJ-child pairs and pE-child pairs ($\chi^2 = 8.644$, df = 1, p < 0.01). It is found that pJ–child pairs are more likely to communicate with each other in the same language(s) than pE–child pairs are.

In order to highlight the differences more clearly, a part of the data from Table B26 (in Appendix B) has been extracted and is rearranged here as Figure 5.28. From this, we can see clearly that when the pJ uses Japanese exclusively (39.2%), the language concordance is rather high: almost all the children use Japanese exclusively as well (37.8%). On the other hand, this is not the case when the pE speaks only in English: the concordance rate is quite a bit lower. While 56.9% of the pEs use English exclusively, only 39.2% of the children do the same. Moreover, the number of children who use both languages to the English-speaking pEs (13.9%) is far greater than that of those who use both languages to

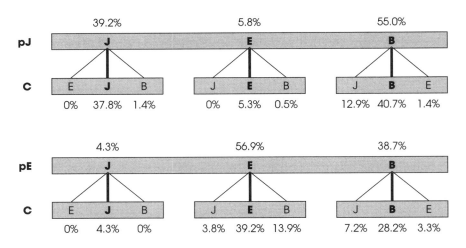

All the numbers in the figure are percentages based on the total number of pJ-C language choice patterns (n=209) and pE-C language choice patterns (n=209)

pJ: parent who is a native speaker of Japanese   pE: parent who is a native speaker of English
C: child   J: Japanese   E: English   B: both Japanese and English

Figure 5.28 Language concordance of parent–child pairs

the Japanese-speaking pJs (1.4%). A few children even use only Japanese to the English-speaking pEs (3.8%), whereas no children use only English to the Japanese-speaking pJs. To the pEs who use both languages (38.7%) in speaking to the children, although most children speak in both (28.2%), more of the remaining children tend to speak only in Japanese (7.2%) than only in English (3.3%). These data suggest a considerable Japanese influence over the language use of the present cross-native/community language families.

As seen above, some children do speak in English in communicating with pEs while others do not. What makes the difference? The next task is to investigate the second research question: under what circumstances is a child likely to speak in the minority-status language to its native-speaking parent? Since the minority-status language here is English, the research question will be restated to reflect this specific focus.

Research question (2): Under what circumstances is a child likely to speak in English to the pE?

Factors

Based on the findings reviewed in Chapter 2, the following factors are examined to identify which ones may most strongly influence the child's use of English to their pE.

Dependent variable
Child's use of English in speaking to the pE
Independent variables: Factor groups and factors

Factor group #1: Parental language use to the child
            Factors: 1. pJ and pE both speaking Japanese
                  2. pJ and pE both speaking English
                  3. pJ speaking Japanese and pE speaking English
                  4. pJ speaking Japanese and pE speaking both languages
                  5. pJ speaking both languages and pE speaking English
                  6. pJ and pE both speaking both languages
Factor group #2: Language/s that the child uses to the pJ
            Factors: 7. English
                  8. Japanese
                  9. Both languages

Factor group #3:   Language/s that the child uses to her/his
                        sibling
        Factors: 10. English
                    11. Japanese
                    12. Both languages
Factor group #4:   The medium of instruction at school
        Factors: 13. English monolingually or bilingually with
                        non-Japanese
                    14. Japanese monolingually or bilingually with
                        non-English
Factor group #5:   Opportunities to play with bilingual friends
        Factors: 15. Some
                    16. Hardly any
                    17. None
Factor group #6:   Gender of the pJ and the pE
        Factors: 18. pE being the mother
                    19. pE being the father
Factor group #7:   Parental perception of bilingualism
        Factors: 20. Beneficial
                    21. Both beneficial and detrimental
                    22. Neither beneficial or detrimental
Factor group #8:   Parental promoting efforts in bilingual
                        child-rearing
        Factors: 23. Yes
                    24. No
                    25. Other
Factor group #9:   Existence of sibling/s and the child's birth
                        order
        Factors: 26. Only child
                    27. First child
                    28. Younger children

Analysis

For the analysis, a variable-rule analysis (Preston, 1989; Rousseau &
Sankoff, 1978; Sankoff, 1988; Young & Bayley, 1996) was performed on
the data, using the GoldVarb Program (Sankoff & Rand, 1990a, 1990b).

GoldVarb is unable to analyze data which include *knockout factors*,
singletons, and *interactive factors*. A *knockout factor* is one for which 'a
certain value of the dependent variable is either always or never present'
(Young & Bayley, 1996: 273). Due to the fact that knockout factors have
categorical effects on variation, the weights of other factors in the factor

group cannot be calculated. A *singleton* is a factor group which includes only one factor. Since there is only one factor in the factor group, there is no need to calculate the weight of that factor. Finally, in order to perform a reliable analysis, GoldVarb requires that factor groups be independent, i.e. not interacting with each other. All factor groups containing these three types of anomalies must be eliminated.

The initial GoldVarb run identified no singletons, but did identify one factor group as being interactive: Factor group #5 (opportunities to play with bilingual friends) was therefore eliminated from the analysis. GoldVarb also found six knockout factors, indicated in Table 5.2 by values of zero in Factor groups #1, #2, #3, #7, and #8. Knockouts do not provide any information on the effects of non-knockout factors in the same factor group. Yet they are worth noting, since their presence in the environment is in itself exploitable information regarding the children's use of language.

In all 12 cases where both parents use English exclusively to the child (Factor group #1), the child uses it when speaking to the pE. In other words, since the pJs in this group are the only pJs who speak exclusively English to the child, it can be said that in all cases where the pJ uses English exclusively to the child, the child also uses English in communicating with the pE. Although not a required condition, due to the fact that the child who uses English to the pE is also found among those to whom the pJ uses Japanese or both languages, the presence of this factor, i.e. the pJ using English to the child (factor 2), allows us to predict the child's use of English to the pE. The same prediction is also made when English is spoken by the child to the pJ (Factor group #2, factor 7) or to her/his sibling (Factor group #3, factor 10). All the children who use English in speaking to the pJ (n = 14) also use it in communicating with the pE. Likewise, all the children who speak in English to their sibling/s (n = 6) use it to the pE as well.

On the other hand, none of the nine children whose parents use Japanese monolingually in speaking to them is found to speak it exclusively to the pE (Factor group #1, factor 1). Since the pEs in this group are the only pEs who speak exclusively in Japanese to the child, it can also be said that in all cases where the pE uses Japanese in speaking to the child, the child uses it to the pE. This may be explained in two ways. The fact that the most likely speaker of English is not using it in speaking to the child not only fails to provide the child with enough exposure but also conveys the message that English is not being promoted at home.

When parents think that being bilingual is neither beneficial nor detrimental (n = 3) (Factor group #7, factor 22), or when they are not actively

Table 5.2 Knockout factors

Factor groups with knockout factors			Number of Cs speaking to pE in:	
			English	Japanese or Both
Factor group #1: Parental language use to the child				
	pJ speaking	pE speaking		
factor 1)	Japanese	Japanese	0	9
factor 2)	English	English	12	0
factor 3)	Japanese	English	25	21
factor 4)	Japanese	Both	3	24
factor 5)	Both	English	45	16
factor 6)	Both	Both	4	50
Factor group #2: Language/s that the child uses to the pJ				
factor 7)		English	14	0
factor 8)		Japanese	37	69
factor 9)		Both	38	51
Factor group #3: Language/s that the child uses to her/his sibling				
factor 10)		English	6	0
factor 11)		Japanese	4	39
factor 12)		Both	28	35
Factor group #7: Parental perception of bilingualism				
factor 20)		Beneficial	81	101
factor 21)		Both beneficial and detrimental	8	16
factor 22)		Neither beneficial nor detrimental	0	3
Factor group #8: Parental promoting efforts in bilingual child-rearing				
factor 23)		Yes	82	104
factor 24)		No	0	12
factor 25)		Other	6	4

pJ: parent who is a native speaker of Japanese
pE: parent who is a native speaker of English
C: child

trying to raise their children to be bilingual (n = 12) (Factor group #8, factor 24), it is not surprising to find that the child does not speak English monolingually to the pE.

After eliminating the five factor groups with knockouts and the one interacting factor group, three factor groups were left for further analysis: #4 (the medium of instruction at school), #6 (gender of the pJ and the pE), and #9 (existence of sibling/s and the child's birth order).

Hypotheses

With the three remaining factor groups (#4, #6, and #9), the following hypotheses were formulated about the factors possibly influencing the child's use of English to the pE.

Döpke (1992a) proposed that the school language has a strong influence on the maintenance of the child's minority language. When the medium of school instruction is the majority language, the minority language of the child is often observed to be negatively affected (Cummins, 1991, 1996; Schmidt, 1991; Wong Fillmore, 1991). On the other hand, when the child's minority language is used at school, its maintenance and further development may be greatly enhanced (Appel & Muysken, 1987). Under such circumstances, the child may be more encouraged to use it at home as well. Hypothesis 1 is thus stated as follows:

> H1: A child who goes to a school where English is used as a medium of instruction is more likely to speak it to the pE than one who does not.

It has been suggested that mothers play an influential role in their children's use of languages. Lük (1986) reported that the bilingual children in his study tended to use the native language of their mother at home. Lyon (1996) also found a strong relationship between the language of the mother and that of the child at an early age. She ascribed this to the mothers having closer relationships with their children than the fathers did. Regarding the gender of a speaker and a child's choice of languages, Hypothesis 2 is formulated as follows:

> H2: A child is more likely to use English to a female pE than to a male pE.

Hoffmann (1985) maintained that having older siblings would increase opportunities for younger children in cross-native/community language families to be exposed to the majority language. Döpke (1992a) also pointed out that the majority language is usually used among siblings.

Döpke claimed that due to the reduced input of the minority language, later-born children tend to be passive bilinguals, in contrast to their older siblings who are more likely to develop into active bilinguals. On the basis of their suggestions, the third hypothesis states:

> H3: Younger siblings are less likely to speak English to the pE than the oldest, who in turn is less likely to do so than an only child.

Results

The final analysis found that only Factor groups #4 and #9 were significant (Table 5.3).

The results show that attending an English-medium school has a promoting effect (0.698) on the child's use of English to the pE, whereas attending a Japanese-medium school exerts an inhibiting influence (0.302) on it, supporting Hypothesis 1.

As for the presence of sibling/s, not having sibling/s has the most favoring effect (0.664) on the child's use of English in speaking to the pE. On the other hand, having sibling/s has an inhibiting influence in the order from younger children (0.368) to the oldest child (0.466). The results support Hypothesis 3.

Table 5.3 GoldVarb results for child's use of English in speaking to the pE

Significant factor groups		*Weight**
Factor group #4: The medium of instruction at school		
factor 13)	English monolingually or bilingually with non-Japanese	0.698
factor 14)	Japanese monolingually or bilingually with non-English	0.302
Factor group #9: Existence of sibling/s and the child's birth order		
factor 26)	Only child	0.664
factor 27)	First child	0.466
factor 28)	Younger children	0.368
	Total Chi-square = 8.6443 df = 4 p < 0.05	
	Chi-square/cell = 0.5403	
	Log likelihood = −129.136	

* Weight measures the influence that each factor has on child's use of English in speaking to the pE, the larger the weight of a factor, the stronger its effects.

The results showed that Factor group #6, the gender difference of the parental speakers, has no significant effect on variation. Thus, no support was obtained for H2, which predicted that a child is more likely to use English to a female pE than to a male pE.

The one parent–one language principle

It has been actively debated whether or not a certain type of parental language use, namely, the one parent–one language principle, promotes children's active bilingual acquisition (Billings, 1990; Döpke, 1998; Lyon, 1996; Romaine, 1995; Shang, 1997). In families adopting a language strategy based on this principle, each parent speaks a different language to the child.

Proponents of the one parent–one language principle claim that it promotes children's active bilingualism. In their monolingual–bilingual comparative study, Bain and Yu (1980), for example, concluded that '[i]f the languages are kept distinctly apart by the parents over approximately the first three and one-half years of the child's life, nativelike control of both languages tends to accrue' (p. 313). Döpke (1998), an enthusiastic proponent of the principle, ensures that 'there is ample evidence that this principle *can* succeed with installing active competence in two languages in young children' (p. 42).

Other researchers, on the other hand, are more cautious about the efficacy of the principle. Romaine (1995) finds that the principle does not necessarily guarantee active bilingualism. Although admitting that some successful cases exist, she argues that '[a] very common outcome of the "one person–one language" method was a child who could understand the languages of both parents, but spoke only the language of the community in which they lived' (p. 186).

Both De Houwer (1990) and Lyon (1996) reserve their conclusions regarding the effects of the principle over bilingual attainment of children. Lyon (1996) did find in her study that all the families who adopted the principle succeeded in raising bilingual children, but they represent only 11% of all the children who attained bilingual competency. With this finding, Lyon (1996) admits that '[i]t is not clear from the present study . . . whether or not the "one person–one language" strategy is the best way to encourage bilingual language development' (p. 212). De Houwer (1990) also expresses her skepticism over the efficacy of the principle, saying that 'so far there is no evidence that other "methods" should fail, be more "difficult" for the child, lead to language delay, or otherwise have disadvantageous results' (p. 54).

Although not clearly articulated in the one parent–one language argument, one underlying assumption is that certain types of parent-to-child language use provide, more than other types, an optimal linguistic environment for promoting the child's use of the minority language, which in turn enhances the likelihood that the child will attain active bilingual proficiency (Figure 5.29).

It can be inferred that proponents of the one parent–one language principle would likely claim that it is the approach which best promotes the child's use of a minority language and is thus the one most likely to result in her/his active bilingual acquisition. On the other hand, those who are more cautious or skeptical about the effect of the principle would probably argue that the one parent–one language approach may not necessarily encourage the child's use of the minority language, and, therefore, her/his active bilingual proficiency may not necessarily be attained.

Since the present study focuses on language use, not language proficiency, it cannot supply any data to examine the second link, i.e. the relationship between the child's language use and enhancement of her/his active bilingual proficiency. Nor can it provide statistical evidence to support or refute the effect of the one parent–one language principle specifically, because the presence of knockout factors prevented the statistical program from calculating the weight of the one parent–one language principle on the child's language use. Notwithstanding these limitations, it is worth examining the descriptive data on the distribution of child language use to the pE in relation to the language use of both parents to the child (Table 5.4).

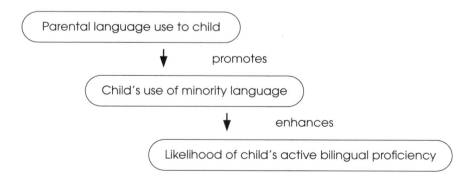

Figure 5.29 Assumed links between parental language use and child's active bilingual proficiency

Table 5.4 Parental language use to the child and the child's language use to the pE

pJ speaking in	pE speaking in	n = 209	(100.0%)		C speaking in English	Both	Japanese
English	English	12	(5.7%)	⇒	12		
Both	English	61	(29.2%)	⇒	45	16	
Japanese	English	46	(22.0%)	⇒	25	13	8
Both	Both	54	(25.8%)	⇒	4	46	4
Japanese	Both	27	(12.9%)	⇒	3	13	11
Japanese	Japanese	9	(4.3%)	⇒			9

pJ: parent who is a native speaker of Japanese
pE: parent who is a native speaker of English
C: child

Among the subject families in the present study, it was found that the pJ using both languages and the pE using English (n = 61 out of the total number of 209, 29.2%) was the most commonly adopted pattern, followed by both parents using both languages (n = 54, 25.8%), and then by the one parent–one language principle, i.e. the pJ using Japanese and the pE using English (n = 46, 22.0%).

Aligning the data in descending order of the ratio of English usage to the whole parental language input and also ascending order of Japanese usage by the pE in parent-to-child interactions, some intriguing patterns seem to appear in the language use of children to the pE. The ratio of English usage to the whole parental language input is assumed to be the highest in the families where both parents use English and the lowest in the families where both of them use Japanese.

According to the data, all the children whose parents both use English in their parent-to-child communication (i.e. the highest ratio of English usage to the whole parental language input and the least Japanese usage by the pE) use English to the pE (n = 12), whereas all the children whose parents both use Japanese in their parent-to-child communication (i.e. the lowest ratio of English usage to the whole parental language input and the most Japanese usage by the pE) use Japanese to the pE (n = 9).

Under the one parent–one language principle, in which Japanese usage by the pE is the least but the ratio of English usage to the whole parental language input is only the midpoint, it was found that, out of 46 children whose parents employ the principle, 25 were speaking to the pE in English monolingually and 21 were not (13 speaking in both languages and 8 speaking in Japanese monolingually).

These data show that, in general, the higher the ratio of English usage to the whole parental language input and the less the Japanese usage by the pE, the greater the likelihood of the child using English to the pE. In other words, the more that both parents use the minority language and the less that the minority language parent uses the mainstream language in speaking to the child, the more likely that the child will use the minority language to the parent who is a native speaker of it.

Because, as stated above, the present study has no data on the child's language proficiency nor on the relationship of language use to proficiency (i.e. whether a lack of active language use necessarily signifies a lack of active language competency), the descriptive data presented here cannot be used as evidence to resolve conclusively the one parent–one language controversy regarding proficiency in the minority language, but they reveal clearly indeed that this principle does not guarantee a child's active use of it.

Summary

The second objective of the present study was to find how languages are used in cross-native/community language families and what factors influence the language use of children in such families.

Regarding the language use of the family members, Total Monolingual Use in English (Type 2) is the most common means of communication between the parents. On the other hand, using both Japanese and English, Total Bilingual Use (Type 9), is the pattern most frequently adopted between the pJ and the children, followed very closely by using only Japanese, Total Monolingual Use in Japanese (Type 1). In contrast, communication between the pE and the children is most likely to be carried out in Total Monolingual Use in English (Type 2). When the children are divided into two subgroups, those with sibling/s and those without sibling/s, we see that, compared to C1-oc–pE pairs, a smaller proportion of child with sibling/s–pE pairs communicate with each other in Total Monolingual Use in English (Type 2). More children in the child with sibling/s group tend to use Japanese in speaking to the pE. In speaking to each other, the largest number of sibling pairs adopt Total Bilingual Use (Type 9), followed very closely by Total Monolingual Use in Japanese (Type 1). Very few pairs of siblings employ Total Monolingual Use in English (Type 2).

Analysis of the children's language use to the pE revealed that the medium of instruction at school and the presence of siblings are influential factors over their use of English to the pE. More children who attend an English-medium school use English monolingually to the pE, whereas more of those who go to a Japanese-medium school speak to the pE either monolingually in Japanese or bilingually in both languages. It was found that children with sibling/s are apt to use only Japanese or both languages to the pE, but those without siblings are likely to speak only in English.

Parental language use to the child and the child's language use to the pJ as well as to her/his sibling were found to have categorical effects on the child's use of English to the pE. Likewise, parental perception of bilingualism and promoting efforts in bilingual child-rearing exert categorical effects over it.

The one parent–one language principle was not the most commonly adopted pattern of language use, and even when it was adopted it did not guarantee the child's exclusive use of English to the English-speaking pE.

Follow-up Interviews

The third main objective was to gain a more microscopic as well as a dynamic view of language use in cross-native/community language families, by obtaining more detailed, in-depth information about their linguistic situations. For that purpose, follow-up interviews were conducted with a small selection of the subject families.

Some of the questions in the questionnaire survey,[3] especially the factual questions including those on language use, were closed questions which, by definition, did not allow respondents much chance to elaborate on their responses. Under what circumstances or on what principles has the family reached decisions on their language use? Is the family satisfied with the choices made, or does the family have regrets or concerns about its chosen course? Follow-up interviews provide opportunities to discuss these issues.

Also, many aspects of family life change over time, for example, the daily schedule of each member, parent–child relationships, and individual interests, to name only a few. In cross-native/community language families, language use among the family members may be one such aspect and may be subject to changes. Conducting follow-up interviews is the best way to discover any major changes, and perhaps also reveal the causes. Six interviews were conducted during the spring and summer of 1998, which was approximately two years after the original questionnaire survey.

Subject families of the follow-up interviews

The subject families selected for interviewing were drawn from a pool of the families who indicated in the original questionnaire their willingness to be future follow-up subjects. Six families were selected because they were exceptionally clear examples of particular types of language use between parents and children (Table 5.5).

The first two families, Family-M and Family-B, use only Japanese for communication in both the pJ–child and the pE–child pairs (Total Monolingual Use in Japanese, Type 1). Conversely, the third family, Family-G adopts English as its exclusive means of communication in the pJ–child as well as the pE–child pairs (Total Monolingual Use in English, Type 2). All three families, though using different languages, present a monolingual language environment in the use of language between the parents and child. The fourth family, Family-S, and the fifth family, Family-C, are ones in which the pJ and the pE each use their own native language in speaking to the child, who in turn speaks in the same language as each parent (Total Monolingual Use in Japanese, Type 1 and Total Monolingual Use in English, Type 2 respectively). Both the pJ and the pE in the sixth family, Family-K, also use their native languages to the child, but the child speaks only Japanese to both parents (Total

Table 5.5 Subject families of the follow-up interviews

	Japanese-only family	English-only family	Japanese-English family	Japanese-oriented family
Subject families	Family-M & Family-B	Family-G	Family-S & Family-C	Family-K
	(Type 1)	(Type 2)	(Type 1)	(Type 1)
pJ speaking to C	J	E	J	J
C speaking to pJ	J	E	J	J
	(Type1)	(Type 2)	(Type 2)	(Type 4)
pE speaking to C	J	E	E	E
C speaking to pE	J	E	E	J

pJ: parent who is a native speaker of Japanese   pE: parent who is a native speaker of English   C: child   J: Japanese   E: English

Monolingual Use in Japanese, Type 1 in the pJ–child pair and Collective Bilingual Use, Type 4 in the pE–child pair). The child is more Japanese-oriented in her/his language use to the parents.

From the individual point of view, the parents and children in all the families conduct parent–child communication monolingually. From the familial point of view, however, whereas Family-M, Family-B, and Family-G each have a monolingual setting, Family-S, Family-C, and Family-K all have bilingual environments.

Family-M: A Japanese-only family

Family-M (see Figure 5.30) is a nuclear family with a mother, a father, and three children (two boys and one girl), living in a busy shopping district in a suburb of Tokyo. The mother in her late forties identifies herself as an Amerasian because she was born in Japan of a Japanese mother and an American father, but grew up in English-speaking environments. After her birth, her family moved to the USA and spent about

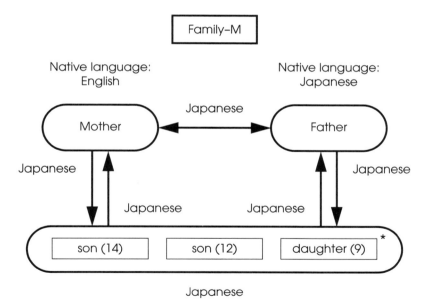

*Ages of the children in the figure are at the time of the questionnaire, and, thus, the ages differ from those discussed in the text because of the real-time lapse. Same for ages in the following figures.

Figure 5.30 Language use in Family-M at the time of the questionnaire

ten years there. The family came back to Japan when her father was stationed at a US Air Force base in Japan. Living on the base, her contacts with Japanese people as well as Japanese language were almost nil.

Throughout high school she received all her education in English on the base. She went to a Japanese college, but enrolled in an international division where the medium of instruction was English. She learned Japanese 'by ear,' listening to the radio, watching TV, or talking with people. She has been in show business in Japan since her college days, and her career also helped her learn Japanese. Her oral Japanese became fluent enough to make her indistinguishable from native Japanese speakers. Due to her lack of formal education in Japanese schools, however, her Japanese writing and reading proficiencies are far less advanced. She used to hold dual citizenship of the USA and Japan, but after marriage, she was naturalized in Japan, assuming that there would not be much possibility of her returning to the USA.

The father is a native Japanese in his early fifties and speaks only Japanese. He is also in show business and has earned fame in Japan. His life is centred around Japan. He does not foresee himself leaving a solid base in Japan behind in order to pursue a career in American show business. His input in decision-making regarding the children's education and language use seems to be minimal, since he entrusted such matters to the mother.

According to the mother's assessment, all the children are monolingual in Japanese. The first son is 16 years old and goes to a Japanese public high school. The second son is 14 years old and goes to a Japanese private junior high school where one-third of the student body consists of foreign students, another third Japanese of 'returnee' students, and the other third of regular Japanese students. Except for English classes, students from all three groups mingle and study together. The medium of instruction at school is Japanese. The daughter is 11 years old and a 6th-grader at a Japanese private elementary school.

The boys used to go to an English-speaking preschool. While they were in preschool, the mother used to speak to them in English and they also responded to her in English. She also made efforts to introduce them to American culture while they were young by celebrating various holidays such as Halloween, Thanksgiving Day, and Christmas. She was planning to have them continue their education in English because she was unfamiliar with the Japanese educational system and her reading abilities in Japanese were not good enough to help them or to deal with the parental paperwork, such as forms, notes, and announcements. At her interview with the principal of an international school in consideration, however, she detected in him prejudiced attitudes towards Japanese people, and this changed her mind. After this incident, she carefully considered her family situation, and came to the conclusion that it would be far more beneficial for her children to establish a firm base in Japanese first, and then master English later. From her own experience she thought that, after all, learning Japanese first and then English later was much easier than the other way around. The family enrolled the boys in a Japanese kindergarten.

Along with changing the course of her children's education, the mother decided to switch her languages and gradually transferred to Japanese when speaking to them. Likewise, the boys stopped speaking in English and started speaking Japanese to her. They very naturally adopted the changes in language use since these occurred in their early days. No confusion or fuss was noticed. The mother thinks that the switch was due to the fact that they had been listening to her speaking in Japanese to other people around them, including the father. Since the switch, their once-developed productive proficiencies in English, if not lost completely, have declined to a minimum. The mother asserts that they understand some English if it is not too difficult. Thus, they must have maintained some passive proficiency, and perhaps even developed it further while listening to the mother speak English to other people.

Except for the period mentioned above, everybody in the family has been speaking only Japanese to each other. All the relatives of both sides who reside in Japan are either monolingual in Japanese or bilingual but they mostly speak in Japanese. Except for their early days at the preschool, all the education of the children so far has been via Japanese. Their friends are all Japanese-speaking as well. The children are totally placed in Japanese environments.

People have pointed out to the mother that she is wasting a good opportunity to raise the children bilingually by not speaking to them in English. She has tried, but the children have rejected English. The children see themselves as Japanese and do not see any necessity to speak English. She respects their feelings. Although she thinks that being able to speak English would widen their horizons, she never pushes them to speak to her in English.

The mother does not object to other families trying to raise their children in two languages simultaneously. Every family is different and has different ways of raising children, she feels. It must be a big task for the parents and must require an optimal environment. It would be wonderful if they succeeded. She takes a position from her own experience, however, that children need a firm base established in one language first. Being exposed to two languages early on is too much for them to handle. They would not be able to pick up everything and neither of their languages would be fully developed. If they want, she thinks, they can learn the other language later, and even do so much faster. She is willing to help her children learn English when they are ready, and feels that the time is just about to come for them.

Family-B: A Japanese-only family

The second Japanese-only family, Family-B (see Figure 5.31), is also a nuclear family with a son and a daughter. In contrast to Family-M, this family lives in a tranquil farming area, several hours by train from Tokyo.

The mother, in her late thirties, is a native speaker of Japanese. She is not working full-time now, but has been teaching Japanese on a voluntary basis to Brazilian children at a nearby junior high school. She was a Chinese major in college and did not like English very much. She has hardly used English in her daily life, so it is difficult to evaluate her English proficiency. When necessary, however, she seems to be able to communicate with people in English to some degree. Around the time when their son was born, the paternal grandmother came from England

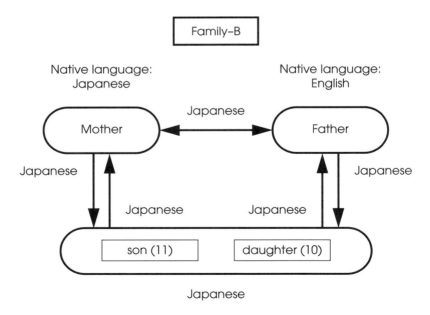

Figure 5.31 Language use in Family-B at the time of the questionnaire

to live with them for a year and the mother managed to communicate exclusively in English with her mother-in-law, who had no knowledge of Japanese.

The father is British in his late forties. His native language is English, but he is extremely fluent in Japanese. He also speaks Chinese. Since childhood he has always been interested in Asia and also in learning other languages, such as Chinese or Japanese. He, thus, has achieved his goals. He teaches English in a junior college not far from his home. Except for his teaching and occasional visits paid by some English-speaking people, the father lives in an almost totally Japanese environment. Even his younger brother, who is now living in England, also used to live in Japan for six years, is also fluent in Japanese, and is also married to a Japanese woman. When the two married couples gather, they end up speaking in Japanese.

All communication among the family members is exclusively in Japanese, except for some occasions when the father speaks English 'just for fun' or says some simple routine expressions, such as 'where did you go today?' In such linguistic environments at home, neither of their children have developed productive abilities in English.

The father thinks that the son, who now is a second year student of a junior high school, barely speaks English, basically due to the lack of his productive abilities. The father claims, however, that when the son does speak English, he can hear his English being qualitatively different from ordinary Japanese students in fluency, pronunciation, speed, and vocabulary. On the other hand, the daughter, who has just started junior high school, seems to reject English. When spoken to in English by the father, she seems to try to evade the situation by 'stalling off.'

The father tries to analyze the two children's differences in attitudes towards English in relation to the differences in their personalities. The son is more adaptable to changes in his environment, whereas the daughter prefers to maintain her familiar environment as it is and tends to avoid any changes in her routine. English may be seen as something that threatens this stable situation in her life. Nevertheless, both of the children seem to have acquired some passive abilities in English, because they can respond in Japanese to what the father says to them in English.

The choice of the family's language use was made consciously, on the basis of some linguistic conditions. First of all, speaking only in Japanese has been the norm of the couple in their communication from the very beginning of their relationship, due to the lack of English fluency on the mother's side. This is the very basic foundation on which the family's language use has been built. In addition, the linguistic environment surrounding the family was a major decisive factor in their language choice. The environment is almost totally Japanese, with hardly any English input around. There are almost no other English-speaking people in their community. The family keeps close-knit relationships with the mother's relatives living nearby. This reinforces the family's Japanese environment. The children even went to the preschool run by their grandmother. The father admits that if they had been living in an area where they were exposed to both Japanese and English more equally, their language use at home might have been different. The family believes that in their circumstances they have made the best choice.

The parents' anxiety regarding their children's psychological well-being also influenced their choice. They are much concerned with possible risks in trying to raise their children to be bilingual. One of the risks they adduce is the development of language disorders, such as stammering, which are allegedly caused by bilingualism. They also pointed out the possibility of under-development in both languages: they were concerned that when two languages are juggled simultaneously, neither of them may develop fully. They believe that establishing one language as a native language first is crucially important. In their case, Japanese was the natural choice for their children. Although they are fully aware of the benefits that English brings to their children, they do not want to overwhelm their children with demands to learn it. They are willing to wait until the children themselves are ready. They understand that it should be natural for many parents of cross-native/community language families to try to raise their children to be bilingual, but what is more important to them is that parents and children have close and meaningful communication with each other in whatever language.

These basic beliefs regarding their children's languages development are reflected in various aspects of their life. Watching foreign shows is one such aspect. Many Japanese–English cross-native/community language families let their children watch English TV shows and videos to reinforce their English abilities. This family also often enjoys British TV shows, movies broadcast on TV, and rental videos. When the shows are bilingually broadcast or recorded, however, they usually watch them in Japanese, which everybody can understand. They try to select shows with subtitles, if possible, so that the father can enjoy them in English while everybody else also can enjoy them. They watch those shows not for the purpose of exposing their children to English, but basically for fun. The mother, however, pointed out that even when translated into Japanese, watching those shows gives their children valuable opportunities to become familiar with British culture.

Another manifestation of their core belief is found in the lack of interest in making trips back to England. Some cross-native/community language families make trips back on a regular basis to the hometown of the non-Japanese parent in order to reinforce their children's second language. Some even enroll their children in a school there during their stay. This family does not seem to be particularly interested in making such trips. The father states that making overseas trips, including visiting England, is not their particular interest. In fact, the family has not been back to England since the last trip six years ago, which was made along with the father's business trip. They think that there are many places to visit and things to do in Japan.

Family-G: An English-only family

Family-G (see Figure 5.32) is an English-only family with two young boys, living in a high-rise in a suburb of Tokyo. The mother is a Briton in her early thirties. She used to be a nurse in her home country, but does not have a full-time job at present. She teaches English on a part-time basis to her neighbors and writes a column for a periodical. Her native language is English and she is able to speak Japanese, French,

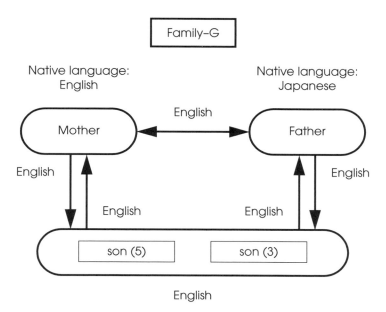

Figure 5.32 Language use in Family-G at the time of the questionnaire

and German as well. She has traveled in many countries all over the world. Although she can manage Japanese fairly well, she pretends in front of the boys that she is less competent in her Japanese than she actually is. She claims that she purposely does not make further improvement to her Japanese, because she believes that her not being good at Japanese will help the boys stay being actively bilingual.

The father is a native speaker of Japanese in his mid-forties and is an architect. Although his English is not good enough to follow native speakers of English without some strain, it is good enough to manage communication within the family. He fully supports English being the only language spoken at home and, in fact, according to the mother, he sometimes promotes it more actively than she does.

The first son is seven years old and has just finished his first year in a public elementary school. According to the mother's evaluation, he is an active bilingual. He can read and write English, although not as well as the children of his age in England. The mother thinks that he is less 'Japanese-oriented' than his younger brother. He actually claims that he feels more comfortable in speaking English than Japanese. The mother notices that the first son sometimes has trouble in Japanese due to gaps in his Japanese vocabulary. Since the mother cannot help him with his school work in Japanese, the parents send him to *juku* (a for-profit school providing supplementary instruction or tutoring) to study Japanese and math. At the same time, in order to maintain a balance in his educational opportunities, the parents regularly order study materials from England which include English language, math, history, geography, and science. The mother helps him study the materials during his summer and spring breaks and other holiday times.

The second son is five years old and is soon to start his last year of kindergarten. In contrast to his elder brother, the younger one is more Japanese-oriented, multi-directionally, from his food preferences to his language proficiencies. He likes speaking Japanese more than English.

The family spends six weeks in England almost every year and enrolls the boys in school/kindergarten or some activities such as a short-time soccer course. Through these activities, their English improves dramatically during their short stay.

Establishing English as a family language was a conscious decision. In addition to her own experiences, the mother has learned through books and presentations on bilingualism that bilingualism does not come naturally. She has become aware that if the family does not work at it, it will not happen. Her understanding is that children may achieve a certain degree of bilingualism at their age level when they are very young, but that the situation may be quite different for school-age children. After children start going to a Japanese school, it is unlikely that they will automatically switch languages when they walk into the house, unless the family sets some rules or establishes certain patterns regarding the use of the languages at home. She also points out that she does not like being placed in a position where she cannot understand what her children are talking about. For these reasons the mother is very strict about English being spoken at home. Although she allows the boys to talk to each other in Japanese to a certain extent, if they go too far, she stops them. She exercises her 'parental authority' to tell them that she will send them to bed unless they switch to English.

The family emphasizes English not only in language use, but also in the identity of the children. The mother says that she has been telling the boys from their early days that they are first English and then Japanese. She explains that in Japan the boys are not identified as Japanese, but as 'foreigners.' She does not want them to grow up believing that they are Japanese, and then later to be hurt by finding out that they are not considered as such by the Japanese people.

Despite her intentions, the mother recently became aware that the boys started talking to each other more in Japanese. This happened, for example, when they were playing together with a Japanese computer game, which is a new addition to their entertainment. This is partly because the game is in Japanese and, thus, it is easier for them to talk about it in Japanese. The mother thinks, however, that more essentially, it is because their Japanese became much stronger in the past few years. According to the mother's observation, the first son's Japanese has become much better, which has influenced the second one's Japanese, which has in turn likewise dramatically improved. The second son is less proficient in English than the first one was at that age. The mother assumes that it is because the first son got much more input in English from her when he was younger. The mother also thinks that the order of birth has some effects on proficiencies in a minority-status language, with the oldest the best, and younger ones less good in it. She does not expect the second son to become fully bilingual.

This change, i.e. the gradual shift towards Japanese, worries the mother, especially since the family is planning to move to England. The family did not have any solid plan to move out of Japan when the original questionnaire was conducted. After the first son started to go to school, however, they began thinking about leaving Japan, partly because they became concerned with the recent increase of criminal incidents at school. When they visited England a couple of years ago, they had the first son take an entrance exam for a private school there, and he passed it. They now know that, although he needs to improve it, his English is good enough to go to school in England. The family is hoping to move to England in a few years.

The mother asserts that bilingual child-rearing is a challenge and a risk. It is such hard work that it even makes her feel that she has to take on two roles, mother and teacher. She does not want to be their teacher, but rather to be their mother. Nevertheless, she thinks that it would be a terrible waste if the boys could not speak both languages. Despite all the parents' efforts, the boys may not develop fully their potential bilingual abilities, but she thinks that they are doing their best for the boys.

Notwithstanding all this, the mother sometimes becomes apprehensive about the path that she and her husband have chosen. Once in a while, she becomes worried that the boys will end up hating to speak in English because of her pressure. She says that she would stop speaking in English to them if their Japanese was suffering or if the pressure to speak English began causing problems, such as behavioral problems at school. She sometimes even wonders whether she should leave them alone now and let them learn English later.

She often discusses the advantages and disadvantages of speaking English at home with the boys. These discussions probably help the boys understand why they are speaking English at home. More than that, they seem to inspire the mother to keep going. The father also encourages her on occasions when she is discouraged.

Family-S: A Japanese–English family

Family-S (see Figure 5.33) is a family in which each parent speaks her or his own native language to the children who, in turn, speak the same language as each parent. The mother, in her early thirties, is a native speaker of Japanese and speaks fluent English. She runs a chain of international preschool/nursery schools at three different locations in central Tokyo. The children in her schools are of 35 different nationalities and many of them are from cross-native/community language families. English is the medium of instruction at these schools, but Japanese is also taught for non-Japanese speakers. The mother's younger sister recently started to work as a teacher at one of her schools.

The father, now in his mid-thirties, came to Japan to study Japanese after graduating from college in the USA. He was planning to stay in Japan for only about six months, but met his future wife, the mother. On their marriage, the father chose to be naturalized in Japan, renouncing his American citizenship. The father's native language is English, but he

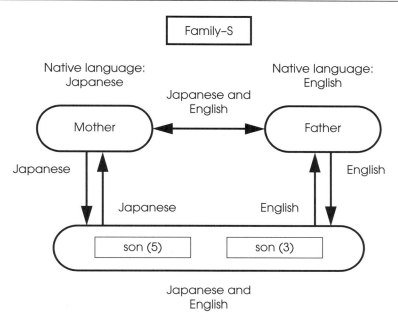

Figure 5.33 Language use in Family-S at the time of the questionnaire

is now fluent in Japanese. His profession is in finance, and he enjoys being with children and lends a helping hand with his wife's schools on weekends. He has a younger brother, who also became interested in Japan and came to Japan to live.

At the time the original questionnaire was conducted, the family had only two boys, but they now have an additional member, an 18-month-old daughter. When the first son, now almost eight years old, was very young, the family spoke only in Japanese. Although the father was not fluent in Japanese at that time, he wanted to provide the son with a Japanese-speaking environment at home, so that the son would be able to acquire full-fledged Japanese. However, when the son was around three, the parents decided to speak to him only in English. According to the mother's recollection, this was due to the fact that the father was frustrated at not being able to express himself well in Japanese.

The son strongly resisted this change. The parents tried to mitigate the son's turmoil caused by this drastic change by having only the father continue to speak in English whereas the mother resumed speaking in Japanese to him. They made great efforts to help the son understand why the father speaks English to him, explaining that the father is an American and English is what he speaks. It helped him to understand the situation and to adapt himself to this new language environment. He is now, according to his mother, a balanced bilingual in English and Japanese. The mother thinks that it is important to teach children each parent's native language.

The first son goes to an international school with English as a medium of instruction, and the parents predict that his English will eventually be much stronger than Japanese. For that reason, they send him to a study *juku* and have him take a few different sports lessons, by which they hope to help him maintain his proficiencies in Japanese. Due to frequent unpleasant experiences with Japanese children, the first son never speaks English when he is alone among other Japanese children.

The second son, almost five years old, attends the mother's preschool as the first son did. Unlike his elder brother, he did not have to go through a drastic change in language use, because the present pattern of language use in the family had been already set when he joined the communication circle of the family. He also speaks both languages, but sometimes mixes languages within one utterance, by replacing some words in one language with their equivalents in the other language.

At the time of the original questionnaire, the boys used both languages between themselves, but now they speak to each other mostly in English. Especially the older one seems to feel more comfortable speaking in English than Japanese. This is probably because he has been exposed to English much more often than to Japanese since he started going to the international school. When speaking to their younger sister, each boy speaks in a different language, with the older one in English and the younger one in Japanese. Although the daughter is still very young, the mother observes that she code-switches, depending on the member of the family: speaking to her mother in Japanese and speaking to all the rest in English.

Despite his earlier intention to stay in Japan permanently, the father has recently become interested in moving back to Hawaii, where he spent his early years. He was first concerned with the children's English not being adequate, but now that they can speak it fluently he feels confident enough to take them there. The mother, on the other hand, is not particularly attracted to the idea of moving to Hawaii, partly because she does not want to abandon her business and partly because she is concerned about the children's education. She hopes that the children, especially the boys, will receive education all the way through high school in an international school in Japan and then go to college wherever they want to.

The mother asserts that the couple are very independent individuals, so that the discrepancy in opinion between them regarding their desires on where to live does not jeopardize their relationship. Even if the father actually decides to move, the couple should be able to work it out. One possible solution, the mother says, would be for her to fly back and forth between the two countries.

The family lives in a residential area with several non-Japanese neighbors in their neighborhood. Many of the Japanese children living in the neighborhood go to private schools, so they do not form play groups, such as are typically found in neighborhoods where most of the children attend the same local public school. As a result, they have little opportunity to play with Japanese-speaking friends in the neighborhood. In addition, the boys go to an international school/preschool, so they have more English-speaking friends from various cultural backgrounds than Japanese friends. The family has been making trips to the USA three times a year, spending in total more than two months out of the year there.

Despite having lived in Japan since birth and having Japanese as one of the languages spoken at home, due to their particular circumstances (i.e. attending English-speaking school, more English-speaking friends than Japanese-speaking friends, frequent trips to the USA), the children seem to have been growing up in an environment that is more English-oriented than Japanese-oriented, both culturally and linguistically. This may be exemplified in an incident that the first son experienced a year before the interview. For about a month and a half during the summer break of the son's school, the parents decided to send him to a local public school to give him an opportunity to receive education in a Japanese school. There he had very different experiences from what he had been familiar with at his own school. Although he did not have any problem in understanding lessons given in Japanese, he was puzzled with the 'jargon' that his peers were using, such as *kireru* (snap) and *mukatsuku* (get on my nerves).

Ways of playing, the other children's behavior, and the school's pedagogy were also all new and strange to him. The mother reports that he was even requested by his teacher not to ask many questions in class, because it disturbed the lessons. The parents also received a letter from the teacher, asking them to guide him to follow his request. In addition to this, he was bullied by other children. All these stressful experiences caused him to develop a stomach ulcer. Although she herself had gone through the Japanese school system, the mother was appalled at the experiences that her son had.

Family-C: A Japanese–English family

Family-C (see Figure 5.34) is another family in which the native language of each parent is spoken in each parent–child communication. The mother, in her late forties, is a native speaker of English from a cosmopolitan city in England. She also speaks Japanese and French. She originally came to Japan to teach English in Tokyo. While she was training to be a teacher in a school in England before coming to Japan, she met her future husband, the father, who was a student in the school. After she came to Japan, they reunited and married. She was teaching English until the first child was born, but now she does not have any paid job. She keeps house and takes care of her two sons, now age 12 and 10. She has been writing a novel in her spare time and is hoping to publish it when it is completed.

The father, a native speaker of Japanese in his early fifties, speaks both English and German, the latter more fluently. He spent five years in Germany with a government agricultural project. He studied German at school and still continues to study it. He is now running his own business as an import coordinator, dealing with German and Japanese

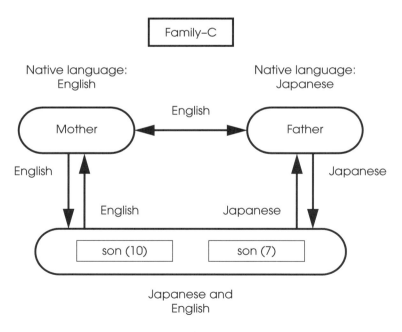

Figure 5.34 Language use in Family-C at the time of the questionnaire

companies. He conducts most of his business transactions by telephone, fax, and computer from an office that he has set up at home. Except for occasional business trips, he spends most of his time in his office at home.

The family lives in a quiet, traditional, rural farming area in the northern part of Japan with the father's parents, in separate houses built side-by-side on the same estate. The couple and the boys used to live in a large cosmopolitan city in the Kansai area. Seven years before the interview, they moved to the present residence to live with the father's parents because the father, being the first son, was expected to do so. The father's parents are farmers and own some rice paddies adjacent to their houses. The couple helps the grandparents with farming.

The family lives in a very traditional community, and it has been rather challenging for the mother to be accepted as a member. She has been making efforts to adapt herself to her new living environment. One such endeavor is to join the boys in a local traditional dancing group. The group practices every week and gives performances in various places. They once performed at Carnegie Hall in New York. She admits that she still feels her Japanese is inadequate, but she has developed a sense of belonging to the community through the activities with the group.

There are no other native English speakers living in their neighborhood except for one American who temporarily resides there, but they hardly socialize with each other. The family, however, receives frequent visits from their friends and guests of different nationalities. In such an environment the boys have been exposed to a variety of languages from time to time.

Until the boys started kindergarten/school, English was the main language at home. Everyone but the father spoke English to each other. The mother asserts that she never forced the children to speak in English but that the pattern just developed naturally. Both boys spoke in English, even to the father who in turn spoke Japanese. The younger one, especially, only answered in English to the father. The father never forced the children to address him in Japanese. After they started kindergarten/school, they began speaking in Japanese to the father more and more while they continued speaking English to each other as well as to the mother.

After the family moved in with the father's parents, the mother recalls that her mother-in-law initially showed her discomfort at the boys' speaking in English. This made the mother tend not to speak English much in front of her. Now that the mother-in-law has realized that the boys speak Japanese fluently and their English is no longer threatening to her, the mother-in-law has relaxed. The mother now does not usually get feelings of disapproval from her any more. The mother never felt any atmosphere of disapproval from the neighbors and now no longer feels it from her mother-in-law, either.

In regard to speaking English, the mother observes that both boys enjoy speaking English. The elder son in particular, now a first-year student at a local junior high school, is very fluent in English, which is often acknowledged by their house guests and visitors. He does not like to show off at school, but enjoys speaking English with his mother. He is actually proud of using it. The younger one, now a fourth grader in a local elementary school, is less proficient. He is sometimes hesitant over his vocabulary and struggles to express himself. None the less, he is not reluctant to speak English. He actually enjoys speaking it and does not intend to give up.

Both boys confirmed the mother's observations. The elder son asserts that he likes speaking English and that it is something quite natural to him. The younger son also affirms that he does not feel embarrassed speaking in English with his mother or his brother, even in front of his Japanese friends, because that is just the way it is. He admits, however, that he feels uncomfortable speaking in English with other people, because they are not his family. He claims that he is happy being able to speak English, because it makes him different from other people. It is no fun to be the same as everybody else. Both boys have had experiences of being bullied by other children, but this never made them abandon speaking English.

The mother observes that the younger son is less proficient in both oral and written English than the older one was at that age. She attributes the differences in their English proficiencies to differences in their personalities. The older one is much more conscientious and serious about everything, while the younger one is 'lazier.' She also thinks that the birth order of children has some effect on their language proficiencies. Younger children tend to have more input in Japanese from their siblings and friends, and thus become more proficient in Japanese and less so in English.

At the time of the original questionnaire, the boys were using both languages between themselves, more or less. However, their use of Japanese has been gradually increasing over the years, and now they speak mainly in Japanese between themselves. The mother recollects that the possible turning point in their language use may have been when the younger son started elementary school; until then, the elder one was still speaking a lot of English to him.

The mother has never felt threatened by this shift in their language use. She expected from the beginning that their Japanese would eventually supersede their English; and thinks it is only natural, since the boys speak Japanese at school every day. She continues trying to maintain their interest in speaking English, but she thinks that it is important that the children speak comfortably whatever language they use. She hopes that the boys have a good enough grounding in English, on which they can keep building more by themselves.

In comparison to their oral proficiencies, their literacy in English is much less developed. The mother used to read English books to both sons every night when they went to bed, which they enjoyed very much. It also helped increase their vocabulary. After the elder son started junior high school, however, he became busier with his homework, which made it very difficult to find time for them to read together regularly, which is a great regret to her. The elder son also regrets it.

The pattern of language use in the family was adopted partly naturally and partly consciously. It just happened that the couple used the language which they felt most comfortable with to each other and they naturally did so to their children as well. They also felt that the mother speaking English to them would be a great means for the children to learn English and that they should try to encourage it. The mother thinks that in any family both parents have to give something of themselves to transmit the whole cultural heritage, and it is impossible to do so without the mother language. She thinks that talking is crucial for success in raising bilingual children. As much as she loves Japan, she is proud of being British, and wants the boys to understand that, and to share in her pride and develop the same feeling themselves.

Family-K: A Japanese-oriented family

In some families the parent-to-child language does not coincide with the child-to-parent one. Family-K (see Figure 5.35) is one such family. The mother is an American in her early forties. Her native language is English. She came to Japan about 20 years ago. While teaching English at various conversation schools, she met her future husband, the father. The father's father (her father-in-law) strongly opposed their marriage, for the reason that the father is from a family with a 500-year lineage and his marrying a non-Japanese would 'mess up' the lineage. The young couple left Japan for Hawaii to have their own family there. After the first child, a daughter, was born, the father-in-law softened and asked them to come back to Japan. He even offered them a house to live in. The mother was not really willing to come back, but eventually agreed to accept his offer, partly because their economic situation in Hawaii was not favorable and partly because she wanted to stay home and raise

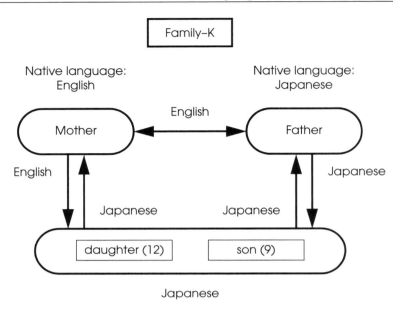

Figure 5.35 Language use in Family-K at the time of the questionnaire

their children. After their return to Japan, the second child, a son, was born.

The mother speaks Japanese fluently now, but her proficiency in writing and reading is very limited. Likewise, the father, now in his mid-forties, speaks English but has poor English literary skills. The mother and the father speak to each other in English. The father uses only Japanese in speaking to the children and so do the children in speaking to him. On the other hand, whereas the mother speaks in English to the children, they use exclusively Japanese to her.

In explaining why the family has adopted this pattern of language use, the mother says that she feels comfortable in speaking her own native language and believes that her children should also feel comfortable in their native language. She does not want to force them to speak English to her. The pattern has remained basically unchanged since the time of the questionnaire survey, but the mother admits that she now tends to speak more Japanese, especially to her son, to make sure that he understands what she says.

According to the mother's observation, the children differ in their comprehension ability in English. She asserts that their daughter, now a 14-year-old junior high school student, understands basically everything she says. On the other hand, she is sometimes uncertain whether their son, an 11-year-old elementary school student, understands what she says to him.

The mother suspects that the differences in their English proficiencies may be ascribed to differences in their personal attributes and life experiences. Their daughter is older and has been exposed to English much more than their son. She was born in Hawaii and lived there until she was one and a half years old. Although both of the children have spent extended periods in the USA during their regular visits, she has made more visits than he has. Being exuberant, she even made a visit to the USA all by herself when she was ten. In addition to those experiences, she once expressed her interest in studying in the USA. The mother believes that although their daughter gets along well with her friends, deep inside she feels the young girls' society in Japan is rather silly and she is uncomfortable with it.

On the other hand, the son, who is the first son of the family, has been raised under the strong influence of the traditional-oriented grandfather and is expected to be 'Japanese.' The mother claims that he is fully aware of this expectation and, likewise, identifies himself as 'Japanese all the way through.' In addition to this identity disposition, after their daughter started school, it became difficult for them to make long trips and, consequently, their son had fewer chances to visit the USA to be exposed to English. The mother also points out that there is less demand on him to use English, since he has an elder sister who can help him by interpreting English into Japanese for him.

The mother accepts the fact that Japanese is the main language of communication at home and says that most of the time it does not bother her. However, she admits that she sometimes becomes 'fed up with having to listen to Japanese all the time.' She claims that she sometimes cannot understand what her daughter says in Japanese when she speaks fast. She divulges that she feels sad about not being able to share many things with her children, such as television programs, movies, or music, because they do not express any interest in English and always prefer Japanese.

Both children play exclusively with Japanese-speaking friends. Although there are opportunities to play with children from a group of other cross-native/community language families, they do not show any interest in those children because they are younger than they are. The son has an American friend of his age in the neighborhood, but does not speak in English to him because the friend, too, can speak fluent Japanese.

As has been described, the linguistic environment that the children have been raised in is strongly Japanese-oriented, and has become even more so, since their mother gradually tends to speak more Japanese to them. The mother was, thus, excited about their daughter starting to take English lessons at school when she began her junior high school. She was hoping that the lessons would enhance her English. To her disappointment, however, the daughter is usually bored with the lessons. In addition, she does not want to speak up in class. The mother thinks that it is partly because she is shy, but it is mostly because the girl is afraid of being bullied if she did. In regard to being bullied, the mother wonders if the hair color of children has something to do with how they are treated by other children. The lighter the color is, the more likely the child is to be picked on. Their daughter actually has lighter-colored hair, while their son has much darker-colored hair and other children do not pick on him. Nevertheless, the children usually amaze other children with their passive bilingual abilities and receive very positive reactions from them. When their friends realize that they understand their mother speaking in English to them, their usual reaction is 'it's cool!'

The mother does not presently worry about their children not speaking English. She believes that if they come to a point in their lives when they want to speak English, their passive abilities will be activated to make them active bilinguals. Her recent experience of their daughter speaking English right away when they arrived in the USA for a vacation made her even more confident in that belief.

Summary

Each family differs in various aspects, such as the parents' proficiency in each other's native language, the accessibility of English resources, the strength of their belief in bilingual child-rearing, and the personality of each family member. These differences doubtlessly contribute to their choice of language to use among the family members.

Some families report that their language choice was consciously made, whereas others claim that it was just naturally set. In whatever way it was settled, every family has experienced or is in the process of experiencing some changes in language use, along with changes in family life as their children grow older. The interviews revealed this dynamic aspect of language use. No family has stood still and every family has been trying to adjust to the changes that they encounter. They are also ready for further adjustment.

Although each family is unique in many aspects, some common observations can be made. One of them was observed in the two families in which only Japanese is spoken between the parents and the children. Both of them expressed concern about possible insufficient development of either language. They are anxious that early exposure to two languages may impose too much pressure on their children and hinder full-fledged development of the languages. They believe that children should establish a firm base in one language first. When their children are ready, they are willing to help them to learn the second language, English.

Another noteworthy point is that most of the interviewees remarked on some differences between the siblings in English abilities or acceptance of English, with the older ones more proficient in English and the younger ones more Japanese-oriented. Each family tried to offer their explanations for the differences as the reflection of differences in the children's personality or in the amount of exposure to each language.

Lastly, most of the families clearly mentioned that they did not want to force their children to speak one language or another. They feel that it is more important for the children to feel comfortable and to communicate with the parents closely and meaningfully in whatever language they like. When the children are ready, they are willing to help them learn the language. Even the mother who is pressing her children to speak English to her claimed that she would stop speaking in English to them if it started to cause them any problems.

Notes

1. Article 14 of the Nationality Law (Law No. 14 of 1950, as amended by Law No. 268 of 1952 and Law No. 45 of 1984), which regulates choice of nationalities, is translated into English as follows:

   Article 14. A Japanese national having a foreign nationality shall choose either of the nationalities
   (a) before he or she reaches twenty-two years of age if he or she has acquired both nationalities on or before the day when he or she reaches twenty years of age; or
   (b) within two years after the day when he or she acquired the second nationality if he or she acquired such nationality after the day when he or she reached twenty years of age.
   2. Choice of Japanese nationality shall be made either by depriving himself or herself of the foreign nationality, or by the declaration provided for in the Family Registration Law in which he or she swears that he or she chooses to be a Japanese national and that he or she renounces the foreign nationality (hereinafter referred to as 'declaration of choice').

2. Hereafter, all cases will be coded according to the following format: [ID#–parent age: C1 sex–age/C2 sex–age/C3 sex–age]. All Japanese expressions in the quotations are Romanized in italics.
3. Although the term *questionnaire* is sometimes used to cover both printed survey questions and those asked in oral interviews (e.g. Giddens, 1997), in this book the former is called a 'questionnaire' and the latter an 'interview.'

Chapter 6
Conclusions

It is often believed that children born and raised in cross-native/community language families will naturally and spontaneously acquire the languages of both parents. The findings in the present study, however, strongly suggest that potential bilingual children in such families are highly influenced by the language of the mainstream society, and that, rather than towards active bilingualism, this influence directs them more towards passive bilingualism, if not total monolingualism in the mainstream language. Under such circumstances, it is unlikely that active bilingualism will be achieved naturally and spontaneously; it must be actively cultivated.

What would be of great interest to cross-native/community language families who are trying to raise their children to be active bilinguals, then, is to find how they can help their children develop the minority language. If we can accept the premise that the more actively we use a language, the further we develop our productive abilities in it, as in the proposed model relating parental language use to child's active bilingual acquisition, then the question may be rephrased as to how parents can promote their children's active use of the minority language.

The present study found two promoting factors for the child's use of the minority language, namely attending an English-medium school and not having siblings, both of which increase the opportunities for the child to be engaged with the minority language. The analysis also revealed that, in general, the more that the parents use the minority language and the less that the minority language parent uses the mainstream language in speaking to the child, the greater the likelihood that the child will use the minority language to the parent who is a native speaker of it. This finding undermines the one parent–one language principle, which does not seem to provide the most optimal linguistic environment for promoting children's active use of the non-mainstream language in cross-native/community language families. The data in the present study showed that the one parent–one language principle was not the most commonly adopted pattern of communication and, even when it was adopted, it did not guarantee the child's exclusive use of the minority language to the parent who is a native speaker of it. Here we detect a strong influence of the mainstream language upon the child's language use.

These findings suggest that a certain principle, which may be termed the principle of 'maximal engagement with the minority language,' is at work. In linguistic environments characterized by this principle, the child receives not only more input of the minority language, but also a subtextual message from the parents that the minority language is expected to be the means of communication in the family. On the other hand, when the minority language parent uses the mainstream language, the child is likely to receive the opposite message, not to mention less input of the minority language. In short, the more engagement the child has with the minority language, the greater her or his likelihood of using it to the minority language parent.

Corroborating the author's previous studies (Yamamoto, 1985, 1987, 1992, 1995), the present results also suggest certain impediments to the children's use of the minority language, namely the conspicuousness of cross-native/community language families. Children born and raised in cross-native/community language families often have to cope with their conspicuousness in the mainstream society, due to the adoption of a language, a pattern of behavior, a life style, and a culture different from those of society at large. When the physical appearance of the minority language parent differs extensively from that of the mainstream group of the society, the conspicuousness extends further, since the children's physical appearance is also likely to be distinctive. Some children may try to minimize their distinctiveness by conforming as best they can to the norms of the mainstream population. One way to conform is to refrain from speaking the minority language.

The study reported on in this book is based on a fairly large sample, by far the largest undertaken in Japan to date. It employed both question-naire and interview methods to obtain not only cross-sectional data but also dynamic views of linguistic situation of interlingual families. The statistical tools available allowed the identification of some factors influencing the children's language use. Notwithstanding all these strengths, the study has some limitations.

One of the limitations regards the sampling procedure. Since all respondents were willing volunteers, the group investigated in the study is not necessarily a random sample of the population. Thus, the findings in the study may not necessarily be generalizable to other families outside the study.

In addition, because the study is limited to the investigation of one particular language group, namely Japanese–English cross-native/community language families, the question also arises as to how well the findings of the present study may be generalized to speakers of other languages. It has been pointed out that the status of a language influences its acquisition and maintenance (Grosjean, 1982; Harding & Riley, 1986) and that English is highly esteemed in Japanese society (Honna, 1995; Kitao et al., 1985). Likewise, bilingualism in Japanese and English is positively evaluated in Japan (Yamamoto, 1998, 2001). Thus, the present subject group may behave quite differently from other language groups in terms of language use and also of attitudes towards bilingualism. Much further research on cross-native/community language families, including those of different language backgrounds, is required before a reasonably complete view can be reached.

Another limitation is that the study did not probe collective language use among family members (e.g. between one parent and a group of children together, between one child and both parents together, or among the whole family members together), instead only focusing on language use between pairs of individual family members (i.e. between parents, between one parent and one child, or between one child and another child). Compared to the patterns of language use between particular pairs, data on collective familial language use may show some shifting when other family members also participate in the interaction.

Lastly, due to this study's methodological limitations, data on children's language proficiencies were not collected; thus, we cannot say whether the children do not actively use the minority language because of their lack of proficiency or for some other reason.

Although the present findings are far from being conclusive, due to the limitations described above, some possible implications may be formulated. First, if attaining bilingualism in the Japanese milieu is neither spontaneous nor easy for speakers of even the most highly esteemed language, then how much more so must it be for the speakers of socially less esteemed languages? Most parents in the present study, hoping that their children will become bilingual in Japanese and English, make efforts to help them to become so, but, as found in the present study as well as in previous studies, not every family experiences success. Considering this, we can only presume that children born into non-English cross-native/community language families are probably even less likely to achieve it.

The second implication is that children in cross-native/community language families are less likely to achieve biliteracy than fluent oral/ aural bilingual abilities. Literacy skills, which require much overt 'teaching,' are usually developed through formal education. Those who attend a Japanese-medium school acquire literacy in Japanese, whereas those who study at an English-medium school, for example, develop literacy in English. The task of teaching children how to read and write in the non-school language is left to the parents, especially to the parent who is a native speaker of that language. In studies on literacy development in cross-native/community language families (e.g. Noguchi, 1999; Swan, 1999), this task has been reported to be painstaking. Literacy training is time-consuming and requires extensive efforts and patience on the part of both parent and child. Not many families can spare that much time and energy for the task.

The interviews showed that the subject families had gone through and were in the process of going through many changes and readjustments in their language milieu and language use. In some families, the pattern of language use had changed according to developments in the family life: a younger child being born, a child starting school, language acquisition or attrition of the family members, the family moving into a different language environment, or developments in the parent–child relationship. It was also suggested that it is subject to more change in the future. Thus, it must be noted that the findings in the present study only reflect one phase in a long process of linguistic adjustment of members of families with two or more languages involved. How languages are used at home is a dynamic process over time, not a fixed state, just as being bilingual is.

The present study does not present any simple and guaranteed ways of raising bilingual children successfully. It is hoped, however, that what the study has revealed will help dispel the folk myths surrounding the phenomenon of bilingualism and thus help families understand what is actually involved in raising bilingual children, so that they can more appropriately cope with the many difficulties which they will certainly encounter in the process.

References

Appel, R. and Muysken, P. (1987) *Language Contact and Bilingualism*. London: Edward Arnold.

Bain, B. and Yu, A. (1980) Cognitive consequences of raising children bilingually: 'One parent, one language'. *Canadian Journal of Psychology* 34 (4), 304–313.

Baker, C. and Prys Jones, S. (1998) *Encyclopedia of Bilingualism and Bilingual Education*. Clevedon: Multilingual Matters.

Billings, M. (1990) Some factors affecting the bilingual development of bicultural children in Japan. *AFWJournal*, April, 93–108.

Byram, M. (1990) Return to the home country: The 'necessary dream' in ethnic identity. In M. Byram and J. Leman (eds) *Bicultural and Trilingual Education* (pp. 77–94). Clevedon: Multilingual Matters.

Celce-Murcia, M. (1978) The simultaneous acquisition of English and French in a two-year-old child. In E. M. Hatch (ed.) *Second Language Acquisition: A Book of Readings* (pp. 38–53). Rowley, MA: Newbury House.

Clyne, M. (1991) *Community Languages: The Australian Experience*. Cambridge: Cambridge University Press.

Clyne, M. and Kipp, S. (1997) Trends and changes in home language use and shift in Australia, 1986–1996. *Journal of Multilingual and Multicultural Development* 18 (6), 443–473.

Crystal, D. (1997) *A Dictionary of Linguistics and Phonetics* (4th edn). Oxford: Blackwell.

Cummins, J. (1991) The development of bilingual proficiency from home to school: A longitudinal study of Portuguese-speaking children. *Journal of Education* 173, 85–98.

Cummins, J. (1996) *Negotiating Identities: Education for Empowerment in a Diverse Society*. CA: California Association for Bilingual Education.

De Houwer, A. (1990) *The Acquisition of Two Languages from Birth: A Case Study*. Cambridge: Cambridge University Press.

De Houwer, A. (1999) Environmental factors in early bilingual development: The role of parental beliefs and attitudes. In G. Extra and L. Verhoeven (eds) *Bilingualism and Migration* (pp. 75–95). Berlin: Mouton de Gruyter.

Deuchar, M. and Quay, S. (1998) One vs. two systems in early bilingual syntax: Two versions of the question. *Bilingualism: Language and Cognition* 1 (3), 231–243.

Döpke, S. (1986) Discourse structures in bilingual families. *Journal of Multilingual and Multicultural Development* 7, 493–507.

Döpke, S. (1992a) *One Parent One Language: An Interactional Approach.* Amsterdam: John Benjamins.

Döpke, S. (1992b) A bilingual child's struggle to comply with the 'one parent-one language' rule. *Journal of Multilingual and Multicultural Development* 13, 467–485.

Döpke, S. (1998) Can the principle of 'one person-one language' be disregarded as unrealistically elitist? *Australian Review of Applied Linguistics* 21 (1), 41–56.

Evans, M. (1987) Linguistic accommodation in a bilingual family: One perspective on the language acquisition of a bilingual child being raised in a monolingual community. *Journal of Multilingual and Multicultural Development* 8, 231–235.

Genesee, F. (1989) Early bilingual development: One language or two? *Journal of Child Language* 16 (1), 161–179.

Giddens, A. (1997) *Sociology* (3rd edn). Cambridge: Polity Press.

Grosjean, F. (1982) *Life with Two Languages: An Introduction to Bilingualism.* Cambridge, MA: Harvard University Press.

Hamers, J. F. and Blanc, M. H. A. (1989) *Bilinguality and Bilingualism.* Cambridge: Cambridge University Press.

Harding, E. and Riley, P. (1986) *The Bilingual Family: A Handbook for Parents.* Cambridge, MA: Cambridge University Press.

Harrison, G., Bellin, W., and Pietre, B. (1977) Bilingual Welsh/English mothers in Wales with special regard to those rearing monolingual (English) children. Report to the Council for the Welsh Language.

Harrison, G. and Piette, A. B. (1980) Young bilingual children's language selection. *Journal of Multilingual and Multicultural Development* 1, 217–230.

Higuchi, T. and Nakamura, T. (1978) Gengo to bunka [Language and culture]. In H. Tanaka (compiled) *Gengo-gaku no Susume* [*Introduction to Linguistics*] (pp.186–231). Tokyo: Taishuukan Shoten.

Hoffmann, C. (1985) Language acquisition in two trilingual children. *Journal of Multilingual and Multicultural Development* 6, 479–495.

Hoffmann, C. (1991) *An Introduction to Bilingualism.* London: Longman.

Honna, N. (1995) English in Japanese society: Language within language. In J. C. Maher and K. Yashiro (eds) *Multilingual Japan* (pp. 45–62). Clevedon: Multilingual Matters.

Huls, E. and Van de Mond, A. (1992) Some aspects of language attrition in Turkish families in the Netherlands. In W. Fase, K. Jaspaert, and S. Kroon (eds) *Maintenance and Loss of Minority Languages* (pp. 99–115). Amsterdam: John Benjamins.

Imedadze, N. (1967) On the psychological nature of child speech formation under condition of exposure to two languages. *International Journal of Psychology* 2 (2), 129–132.

Iritani, T. (1988) *Gengo-Shinri-gaku no Susume* [*Introduction to Psycholinguistics*]. Tokyo: Taishuukan Shoten.

Japan Council of International Schools/Ministry of Education, Science, Sports and Culture (1994) *Outline of International Schools in Japan 1994.* Tokyo: Japan Council of International Schools/Ministry of Education, Science, Sports and Culture.

Japan Immigration Association (1996) *Statistics on Immigration Control, 1995.* Tokyo: Japan Immigration Association.

Kim, D. (1991) Zainichi chousenjin-shijo no bairingarizumu [Bilingualism among Korean youth residing in Japan]. In J. C. Maher and K. Yashiro (eds) *Nihon no Bairingarizumu* [*Bilingualism in Japan*] (pp. 125–148). Tokyo: Kenkyuusha Shuppan.

Kitao, S. K., Kitao, K., Nozawa, K., and Yamamoto, M. (1985) Teaching English in Japan. In K. Kitao (compiled) *TEFL in Japan: A Compendium to Commemorate the 10th Anniversary of the Japan Association of Language Teachers* (pp. 297–305). Kyoto: The Japan Association of Language Teachers. (ERIC Document Reproduction Service NO. ED 265 741.)

Kokuritsu Shakai Hoshou Jinkou-Mondai Kenkyuusho (ed.) (1998) *Jinkou no Doukou: Nihon to Sekai* [*Population Trends: Japan and the World*]. Tokyo: Kousei Toukei Kyoukai.

Lanza, E. (1992) Can bilingual two-year-olds code-switch? *Journal of Child Language* 19 (3), 633–658.

Lanza, E. (1997) *Language Mixing in Infant Bilingualism: A Sociolinguistic Perspective.* New York: Oxford University Press.

Leopold, W. F. (1939–1949) *Speech Development of a Bilingual Child: A Linguist's Record* (4 vols). Evanston, IL: Northwestern University Press. (Reprinted in 1970 by AMS Press, New York.)

Leopold, W. F. (1978) A child's learning of two languages. In E. M. Hatch (ed.) *Second Language Acquisition* (pp. 23–32). Rowley, MA: Newbury House. (Reprinted from *Georgetown University Round Table on Languages and Linguistics*, 1954, 7, 19–30.)

Lindholm, K. J. and Padilla, A. M. (1978) Language mixing in bilingual children. *Journal of Child Language* 5, 327–335.

Lük, A. N. (1986) Mother tongue and national identity of children from mixed marriages in a bilingual setting. *Grazer Linguistische Studien* 27, Fall, 103–112.

Lyon, J. (1996) *Becoming Bilingual: Language Acquisition in a Bilingual Community.* Clevedon: Multilingual Matters.

Lyon, J. and Ellis, N. (1991) Parental attitudes towards the Welsh language. *Journal of Multilingual and Multicultural Development* 12 (4), 239–252.

McCarty, S. (1999) Ni-gengo · ni-bunka heiyou no igi: Seijin bairingaru no jiko kansatsu [The meaning of being bilingual and bicultural: Self-observations of adult bilinguals]. In M. Yamamoto (ed.) *Bairingaru no Sekai* [*The World of the Bilingual*] (pp. 133–159). Tokyo: Taishuukan Shoten.

Maher, J. C. and Honna, N. (eds) (1994) *Atarashii nihon-kan sekai-kan ni mukatte: Nihon ni okeru gengo to bunka no tayousei* [*Towards a New Order: Language and Cultural Diversity in Japan*]. Tokyo: Kokusai Shoin.

Maher, J. C. and Yashiro, K. (1995) *Multilingual Japan.* Clevedon: Multilingual Matters.

Meisel, J. M. (1989) Early differentiation of languages in bilingual children. In K. Hyltenstam and L.K. Obler (eds) *Bilingualism across the Lifespan: Aspects of Acquisition, Maturity, and Loss* (pp. 13–40). Cambridge: Cambridge University Press.

Milroy, L. and Muysken, P. (1995) *One Speaker, Two Languages: Cross-Disciplinary Perspectives on Code-Switching.* Cambridge: Cambridge University Press.

Ministry of Education, Science, Sports and Culture (1992) Nihongo Kyouiku ga Hitsuyouna Gaikokujin-Jidou · Seito no Ukeire · Shidou no Joukyou ni tsuite [1991 Report on Conditions for Foreign Students Requiring Japanese Language Education]. Tokyo: Ministry of Education, Science, Sports and Culture.

Ministry of Education, Science, Sports and Culture (1994) 'Heisei 5-nen-do Nihongo Kyouiku ga Hitsuyouna Gaikokujin-Jidou · Seito no Ukeire Joukyou tou-ni kansuru Chousa' no Kekka [1993 Report on Conditions for Foreign Students Requiring Japanese Language Education]. Tokyo: Ministry of Education, Science, Sports and Culture.

Ministry of Education, Science, Sports and Culture (1996) 'Heisei 7-nen-do Nihongo Kyouiku ga Hitsuyouna Gaikokujin-Jidou · Seito no Ukeire Joukyou tou-ni kansuru Chousa' no Kekka [1995 Report on Conditions for Foreign Students Requiring Japanese Language Education]. Tokyo: Ministry of Education, Science, Sports and Culture.

Ministry of Education, Science, Sports and Culture (1997) Kodomo no Gakushuu-hi Chousa Houkokusho [Report on Children's Educational Expenses]. Tokyo: Ministry of Education, Science, Sports and Culture.

Ministry of Education, Science, Sports and Culture (1998) 'Heisei 9-nen-do Nihongo Kyouiku ga Hitsuyouna Gaikokujin-Jidou · Seito no Ukeire Joukyou tou-ni kansuru Chousa' no Kekka [1997 Report on Conditions for Foreign Students Requiring Japanese Language Education]. Tokyo: Ministry of Education, Science, Sports and Culture.

Ministry of Education, Science, Sports and Culture (2000) 'Heisei 11-nen-do Nihongo Kyouiku ga Hitsuyouna Gaikokujin-Jidou Seito no Ukeire Joukyou tou-ni kansuru Chousa' no Kekka [1999 Report on Conditions for Foreign Students Requiring Japanese Language Education]. Tokyo: Ministry of Education, Science, Sports and Culture.

Moon, L. (1991) Foreign cross-cultural moms prefer Japanese schools for their children. The Japan Times, 31 March, p. 12.

Noguchi, M. G. (1999) Katei deno dokuji shidou wa kanou-ka: 22 kazoku ni miru seikou no youin [Is it possible to teach reading at home?: Factors for success found in a survey of 22 families]. In M. Yamamoto (ed.) Bairingaru no Sekai [The World of the Bilingual] (pp. 33–63). Tokyo: Taishuukan Shoten.

Noguchi, M. G. and Fotos, S. (2001) Studies in Japanese Bilingualism. Clevedon: Multilingual Matters.

Oka, H. (1989) Bringing up children bilingually in Japan. Studies in English Language and Literature 39, 113–132.

Pan, B. A. (1995) Code negotiation in bilingual families: 'My body starts speaking English'. Journal of Multilingual and Multicultural Development 16 (4), 315–327.

Paradis, M. (1998) Neurolinguistic aspects of the native speaker. In R. Singh (ed.) The Native Speaker: Multilingual Perspectives (pp. 205–219). New Delhi: Sage.

Pattayanak, D. P. (1998) Mother tongue: An Indian context. In R. Singh (ed.) The Native Speaker: Multilingual Perspectives (pp. 124–147). New Delhi: Sage.

Paulston, C. B. (1994) Linguistic Minorities in Multilingual Settings. Amsterdam: John Benjamins.

Pauwels, A. F. (1985) The role of mixed marriages in language shift in the Dutch communities. In M. G. Clyne (ed.) Australia, Meeting Place of Languages (Pacific Linguistics C92) (pp. 39–55). Canberra: Dept of Linguistics, Research School of Pacific Studies.

Peal, E. and Lambert, W. E. (1962) The relation of bilingualism to intelligence. Psychological Monographs: General and Applied 76 (27), 1–23.

Preston, D. R. (1989) Sociolinguistics and Second Language Acquisition. New York: Basil Blackwell.

Pye, C. (1986) One lexicon or two?: An alternative interpretation of early bilingual speech. *Journal of Child Language* 13, 591–593.

Richards, J., Platt, J., and Weber, H. (1985) *Longman Dictionary of Applied Linguistics*. Essex: Longman.

Romaine, S. (1995) *Bilingualism*. Oxford: Basil Blackwell.

Rousseau, P. and Sankoff, D. (1978) Advances in variable rule methodology. In D. Sankoff (ed.) *Linguistic Variation: Models and Methods* (pp. 57–69). New York: Academic Press.

Sankoff, D. (1988) Variable rules. In U. Ammon, N. Dittmar, and K. J. Mattheier (eds) *Sociolinguistics: An International Handbook of the Science of Language and Society* (pp. 984–997). Berlin: de Gruyter.

Sankoff, D. and Rand, D. (1990a) *GoldVarb Version 2: A Variable Rule Application for the Macintosh*™ (computer program). Montréal: Université de Montréal.

Sankoff, D. and Rand, D. (1990b) *GoldVarb Version 2: A Variable Rule Application for the Macintosh*™ (computer program manual). Montréal: Université de Montréal.

Saunders, G. (1982) *Bilingual Children: Guidance for the Family*. Clevedon: Multilingual Matters.

Schaerlaekens, A., Zink, I., and Verheyden, L. (1995) Comparative vocabulary development in kindergarten classes with a mixed population of monolinguals, simultaneous and successive bilinguals. *Journal of Multilingual and Multicultural Development* 16 (6), 477–495.

Schmidt, A. (1991) Language attrition in Boumaa Fijian and Dyirbal. In H. W. Seliger and R. M. Vago (eds) *First Language Attrition* (pp. 113–124). Cambridge: Cambridge University Press.

Shang, S. (1997) Raising bilingual/bicultural children in Kyushu: A survey. *Research Bulletin of Kagoshima Women's College* 18 (2), 43–58.

Singh, R. (ed.) (1998) *The Native Speaker: Multilingual Perspectives*. New Delhi: Sage.

Skutnabb-Kangas, T. (1981) *Bilingualism or Not: The Education of Minorities*. Clevedon: Multilingual Matters.

Skutnabb-Kangas, T. (2000) *Linguistic Genocide in Education – Or Worldwide Diversity and Human Rights?* Mahwah, NJ: Lawrence Erlbaum.

Smolicz, G. (1981) Core values and ethnic identity. *Ethnic and Racial Studies* 4, 75–90.

Soumu-chou Seishounen Taisaku Honbu (1996) Kodomo to Kazoku ni kansuru Kokusai Hikaku Chousa Houkokusho [Report on a Comparative International Study of Children and Their Families]. Tokyo: Soumu-chou Seishounen Taisaku Honbu.

Statistics and Information Department, Minister's Secretariat, Ministry of Health and Welfare (ed.) (1994) *Vital Statistics of Japan: 1992* (Vol. 1). Tokyo: Health and Welfare Statistical Association.

Statistics and Information Department, Minister's Secretariat, Ministry of Health and Welfare (ed.) (1995) *Vital Statistics of Japan: 1993* (Vol. 1). Tokyo: Health and Welfare Statistical Association.

Statistics and Information Department, Minister's Secretariat, Ministry of Health and Welfare (ed.) (1996) *Vital Statistics of Japan: 1994* (Vol. 1). Tokyo: Health and Welfare Statistical Association.

Statistics and Information Department, Minister's Secretariat, Ministry of Health and Welfare (ed.) (1997) *Vital Statistics of Japan: 1995* (Vol. 1). Tokyo: Health and Welfare Statistical Association.

Statistics and Information Department, Minister's Secretariat, Ministry of Health and Welfare (ed.) (1998) _Vital Statistics of Japan: 1996_ (Vol. 1). Tokyo: Health and Welfare Statistical Association.

Statistics and Information Department, Minister's Secretariat, Ministry of Health and Welfare (ed.) (1999) _Vital Statistics of Japan: 1997_ (Vol. 1). Tokyo: Health and Welfare Statistical Association.

Statistics Bureau, Management and Coordination Agency (ed.) (1993) _Japan Statistical Yearbook: The 43rd Edition (1994)_. Tokyo: Japan Statistical Association.

Statistics Bureau, Management and Coordination Agency (ed.) (1996) _Japan Statistical Yearbook: The 46th Edition (1997)_. Tokyo: Japan Statistical Association.

Statistics Bureau, Management and Coordination Agency (ed.) (1997) _Japan Statistical Yearbook: The 47th Edition (1998)_. Tokyo: Japan Statistical Association.

Statistics Bureau, Management and Coordination Agency (ed.) (1998) _Japan Statistical Yearbook: The 48th Edition (1999)_. Tokyo: Japan Statistical Association.

Statistics Bureau, Management and Coordination Agency (ed.) (1999) _Japan Statistical Yearbook: The 49th Edition (2000)_. Tokyo: Japan Statistical Association.

Suzuki, T. (1975) _Tozasareta Gengo: Nihongo no Sekai_ [_Closed Language: The World of Japanese_]. Tokyo: Shinchousha.

Swan, J. (1999) Kodomo no yomu-nouryoku no hattatsu katei: Bairingaru shitei no souiten to kyoutsuuten [The developmental process of children's reading ability: Differences and similarities between two bilingual children]. In M. Yamamoto (ed.) _Bairingaru no Sekai_ [_The World of the Bilingual_] (pp. 100–132). Tokyo: Taishuukan Shoten.

Taeschner, T. (1983) _The Sun is Feminine: A Study on Language Acquisition in Bilingual Children_. Berlin: Springer-Verlag.

Toyama, S. (1974) _Josei no Ronri_ [_Women's Logic_]. Tokyo: Chuuou Kouronsha.

Vihman, M. M. (1985) Language differentiation by the bilingual infant. _Journal of Child Language_ 12, 297–324.

Vihman, M. M. (1986) More on language differentiation. _Journal of Child Language_ 13, 595–597.

Volterra, V. and Taeschner, T. (1978) The acquisition and development of language by bilingual children. _Journal of Child Language_ 5, 311–326.

Winsler, A., Díaz, R. M., Espinosa, L., and Rodríguez, J. L. (1999) When learning a second language does not mean losing the first: Bilingual language development in low-income, Spanish-speaking children attending bilingual preschool. _Child Development_ 70 (2), 349–362.

Wong Fillmore, L. (1991) When learning a second language means losing the first. _Early Childhood Research Quarterly_ 6, 323–346.

Yamamoto, M. (1985) Nihon no bairingaru-tachi: Ankeito chousa ni yoru eigo-nihongo bairingaru no gengo kankyou kousatsu [Bilinguals in Japan: A study of the linguistic environments of English-Japanese bilinguals – A questionnaire survey]. In F. C. Peng, K. Akiyama, and M. Hamada (eds) _Shakai no naka no Gengo: Kigou, Ningen, Kankyou no Sougo Sayou_ [_Language in Society: The Interactions of Linguistic Code, Humans, and Environment_] (pp. 161–184). Hiroshima: Bunka Hyouron Shuppan.

Yamamoto, M. (1987) Significant factors for raising children bilingually in Japan. _The Language Teacher_ 11 (10), 17–23.

Yamamoto, M. (1991) _Bairingaru_ [_Bilinguals_]. Tokyo: Taishuukan Shoten.

Yamamoto, M. (1992) Linguistic environments of bilingual families in Japan. *The Language Teacher* 16 (5), 13–15.

Yamamoto, M. (1995) Bilingualism in international families. In J. C. Maher and K. Yashiro (eds) *Multilingual Japan* (pp. 63–85). Clevedon: Multilingual Matters.

Yamamoto, M. (1996) *Bairingaru-wa donoyounishite Gengo-wo Shuutoku suru-no-ka [How Bilinguals Acquire Their Languages]*. Tokyo: Akashi Shoten.

Yamamoto, M. (1998) A survey on perception of 'bilinguals': What the results imply. *The Japanese Journal of Language in Society* 1 (1), 11–18.

Yamamoto, M. (2000) Language use in Japanese-English interlingual families: A sociolinguistic study of families with two different mother tongues. Doctoral dissertation, International Christian University, Tokyo.

Yamamoto, M. (2001) Japanese attitudes towards bilingualism: A survey and its implications. In M. G. Noguchi and S. Fotos (eds) *Studies in Japanese Bilingualism* (pp. 24–44), Clevedon: Multilingual Matters.

Yim, Y. C. (1993) *Zainichi · Zaibei Kankoku-jin oyobi Kankoku-jin no Gengo Seikatsu no Jittai [Language Life of Koreans, Korean-Japanese and Korean-Americans]*. Tokyo: Kuroshio Shuppan.

Yoshioka, J. G. (1929) A study of bilingualism. *Journal of Genetic Psychology* 36, 473–479.

Young, R. and Bayley, R. (1996) VARBRUL Analysis for second language acquisition research. In R. Bayley and D. R. Preston (eds) *Second Language Acquisition and Linguistic Variation* (pp. 253–306). Amsterdam: John Benjamins.

Appendix A

LANGUAGE USE IN BILINGUAL FAMILIES QUESTIONNAIRE

The purpose of this questionnaire is to investigate language use among members of "bilingual families". I would be grateful if you would cooperate by filling it out.

There are two equivalent versions of the questionnaire: an English one (blue paper) and a Japanese one (pink paper). I regret that I am unable to provide other language versions. Please fill out only the one which you feel most comfortable with, but please return both versions in the enclosed envelope. Postage is not necessary.

The organization of the questionnaire is as follows:

I. FAMILY BACKGROUND (Q1~Q2)
II. FAMILY'S LINGUISTIC SITUATION
    A. Language Use among Family Members (Q3~Q4)
    B. Children's Language Use at Play (Q5)
    C. Language(s) Used for Instruction at School (Q6)
    D. The Place Where You Live (Q7~Q9)
III. ATTITUDES AND PERCEPTIONS ABOUT BILINGUALISM (Q10~Q14)
IV. PROMOTION OF BILINGUALISM (Q15)

Who are your family members?

(1) What persons are now living in your household? Please check every appropriate box. Indicate the total number of children you have, whether they are presently living with you or not.

(2) Which person is filling out this questionnaire? Please circle the picture that represents you.

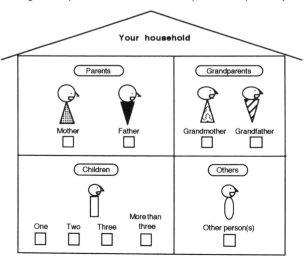

I. FAMILY BACKGROUND

Q 1 Please fill in CHART 1, regarding the sex, age, nationality, residence, and language of each family member.

[1] In case of multiple nationality, please list each.

[2] If more than one language is considered to be "native," please list each.

CHART 1	Sex	Age	[1] Nationality	Current residence	Language(s) [2] Native language(s)	Language(s) Other language(s) that s/he can use
(E.g.) Child 1	F M	18	Japan, Canada	Japan	English, Japanese	French
Mother						
Father						
Child 1	F M					
Child 2	F M					
Child 3	F M					
Grand-mother						
Grand-father						

If there are other family members living in your household, please add them here.

Q 2 Where has your family lived since the first child was born?

CHART 2		
Duration	Location	What languages are mainly used in those areas?
(E.g.) 1986−1990 1990−present	Toronto (Canada) Yokohama (Japan)	English Japanese

II. FAMILY'S LINGUISTIC SITUATION

A. Language Use among Family Members

Q 3 What languages are generally used among your family members? Please fill in CHART 3, as the example below shows. If more than one language is used, please circle the most frequently used language(s).

┌ English and Japanese are most frequently used.

(E.g.)	Mother	Father	Child 1	Child 2	Child 3	Grand-mother	Grand-father
Mother →		English	English Japanese French	English Japanese	Japanese	Japanese	

└ English is most frequently used.

CHART 3							
The speaker	**The person spoken to**						
	Mother	Father	Child 1	Child 2	Child 3	Grand-mother	Grand-father
Mother →							
Father →							
Child 1 →							
Child 2 →							
Child 3 →							
Grandmother →							
Grandfather →							

If there are other family members living in your household, please add them here.

Q 4 Do you ever mix languages in the same sentence when speaking to each other?
(E.g.: It's MENDOKUSAI, but I've got to do it.) Please check only one box for each person.

CHART 4	never do it	sometimes do it	often do it	always do it	do not know
Mother	☐	☐	☐	☐	☐
Father	☐	☐	☐	☐	☐
Child 1	☐	☐	☐	☐	☐
Child 2	☐	☐	☐	☐	☐
Child 3	☐	☐	☐	☐	☐
Grandmother	☐	☐	☐	☐	☐
Grandfather	☐	☐	☐	☐	☐

If there are other family members living in your household, please add them here.

B. Children's Language Use at Play

Q 5 How often do your children play with: (1) children who speak only Japanese; (2) children who do not speak Japanese; and (3) children who speak both Japanese and (an)other language(s)?
Please check only one box for each item.

CHART 5	(1) children who speak only Japanese	(2) children who do not speak Japanese	(3) children who speak both Japanese and (an)other language(s)
Child 1	☐ often ☐ sometimes ☐ hardly ever / never	☐ often ☐ sometimes ☐ hardly ever / never	☐ often ☐ sometimes ☐ hardly ever / never
Child 2	☐ often ☐ sometimes ☐ hardly ever / never	☐ often ☐ sometimes ☐ hardly ever / never	☐ often ☐ sometimes ☐ hardly ever / never
Child 3	☐ often ☐ sometimes ☐ hardly ever / never	☐ often ☐ sometimes ☐ hardly ever / never	☐ often ☐ sometimes ☐ hardly ever / never

If there are more children, please use this space to answer the questions for each of them.

C. Language(s) Used for Instruction at School

Q 6 Please fill in CHART 6, regarding your children's school enrollment and medium of instruction.

$^{1)}$ Regarding "Enrollment," please circle only one choice for each child. If the child attends kindergarten or preschool, please choose "in school now". If the child is "in school now," please answer all other questions as well.

$^{2)}$ "Type of school" are such divisions as "Japanese public school," "Japanese private school," "International school," "Mission school," etc.

$^{3)}$ "Level of school" are such divisions as "Elementary school," "Junior high school," etc. Please choose an appropriate one from the list below:

> Preschool, Kindergarten, Elementary school, Junior high school, Senior high school, Junior college, College/University, Graduate school, Vocational school, Other (Please specify in the optional space below.)

(E.g.)	$^{1)}$ Enrollment	$^{2)}$ Type of school	$^{3)}$ Level of school	Grade	Medium of Instruction
Child 1	not yet in school				
	in school now ➡	Japanese private school	Junior high school	2nd	Japanese
	already out of school				

CHART 6	$^{1)}$ Enrollment	$^{2)}$ Type of school	$^{3)}$ Level of school	Grade	Medium of Instruction
Child 1	not yet in school				
	in school now ➡				
	already out of school				
Child 2	not yet in school				
	in school now ➡				
	already out of school				
Child 3	not yet in school				
	in school now ➡				
	already out of school				
If there are more children, please use this space to answer the questions for each of them.					

D. The Place Where You Live

Q 7 In which of the following areas do you now reside? Please check one box each for A and B. If none of them is appropriate, please check "other" and elaborate your answer.

A : ☐ inner city ☐ suburb ☐ other: _____

B : ☐ residential area ☐ farming area ☐ factory area ☐ other: _____

Q 8 Are there many opportunities for your family to meet non-Japanese speakers in the area where you reside now?

☐ many ☐ some ☐ few ☐ none

Q 9 Do you plan to move to a non-Japanese-speaking area in the near future?

☐ No ☐ Yes ➡ What language is spoken there? : _____

III. ATTITUDES AND PERCEPTIONS ABOUT BILINGUALISM

Q 10 Do you and your spouse think being bilingual is beneficial or detrimental? (You need not to consider "reading/writing" abilities here.) Please check the appropriate box and describe the reason.

CHART 7	Why?
☐ beneficial	
☐ detrimental	
☐ both	
☐ neither	

Q 11 What do you think is the general Japanese perception of bilinguals who speak your and your spouse's native languages? Please check the appropriate box.

very positive	somewhat positive	neutral	somewhat negative	very negative
☐	☐	☐	☐	☐

Q 12 Do you think bilinguals speaking other combinations of languages are perceived the same way in Japan? Please check the appropriate box and give the reason.

CHART 8	
☐ Yes	Why?
☐ No	Why not?

Q 13 Have you and/or your spouse ever encountered any sort of negative reaction from your children when speaking to them in a language other than Japanese in the presence of their Japanese friends?

CHART 9
☐ Yes   Please describe the situations(s) and what you or your spouse did on those occasions:
☐ No   Comments, if any:

Q 14 Have your children ever experienced anything, either desirable or undesirable, which seemed to be due to the fact that they were born and raised in a bilingual family?

CHART 10
☐ No, at least not that we know of
☐ Yes   ☐ experienced something desirable   Please explain:
☐ experienced something undesirable   Please explain:

IV. PROMOTION OF BILINGUALISM

Q 15 Are you and your spouse trying to raise your children to be bilingual? (You need not to consider "reading/writing" abilities here.) Please check the appropriate box and elaborate your answers.

CHART 11	
☐ Yes	Why? How?
☐ No	Why not?
☐ Other	Please explain:

— — — — — — **Thank you very much for your cooperation** — — — — — —

In addition to this questionnaire, I'd like to conduct follow-up interviews. If your family is willing to be interviewed, please give your contact information in the space below.

YOUR PRIVACY WILL BE RESPECTED

Your name : _____

Address : _____

Phone : _____

バイリンガル家族の言語使用
アンケート調査

> このアンケート調査は「バイリンガル家族」の言語使用の状況を調べるために行うものです。ご協力いただけましたら幸いに存じます。
> アンケート用紙は、日本語版（ピンク）と英語版（ブルー）の2種類を用意しました。他の言語によるものは、諸般の事情により準備することができませんでした。どうぞご了承下さい。どちらの版も内容は同じですので、<u>読みやすい方を1つだけ選び、ご回答の上、使用されなかった方の版と一緒に、同封の封筒にてご返送下さい。切手は不要ですので、そのままご投函下さい。</u>

このアンケートは、次のような構成になっています

> I. 家族の背景 (Q1〜Q2)
> II. 家族の言語状況
>   A. 家族構成員間における言語使用 (Q3〜Q4)
>   B. 遊びにおける言語使用 (Q5)
>   C. 学校の授業で用いられている言語 (Q6)
>   D. 居住地 (Q7〜Q9)
> III. バイリンガリズムに対する態度と認識 (Q10〜Q14)
> IV. バイリンガリズムの奨励 (Q15)

- -

あなたの家族にはどなたがいますか

(1) 現在、同一世帯で暮らしている人はだれですか。その人たちすべての□の中に×の印を入れて下さい。<u>子どもについては、現在、同居している、いないにかかわりなく、全員の人数を示す□の中に×の印を入れて下さい。</u>

(2) このアンケートに答えて下さるのはどなたですか。その方を示す絵を○で囲んで下さい。

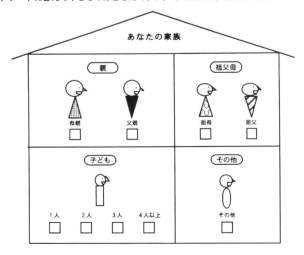

I. 家族の背景

Q1 家族を構成する人々の性別、年齢、国籍、居住地、言語を表1の各欄に記入して下さい。

1) 多重国籍を持つ人については、その国名すべてを記入して下さい。

2) 母語が複数あると考える場合には、それらすべてを記入して下さい。

表 1	性別	年齢	1) 国籍	現在の居住地	言語	
					2) 母語	その他に使用できる言語
(例) 子ども 1	女 男	18	日本、カナダ	日本	日本語、英語	フランス語
母親						
父親						
子ども 1	女 男					
子ども 2	女 男					
子ども 3	女 男					
祖母						
祖父						

もしこの他に同居している家族がいれば、ここに追加記入して下さい。

Q2 最初の子どもが生まれてから今日まで、あなたの家族はどこに居住してきましたか。

表 2		
居住していた期間	居住していた場所	それらの地域では何語が主に話されていますか
(例) 1986－1990 1990－現在	トロント（カナダ） 横浜（日本）	英語 日本語

II.　家族の言語状況

A.　家族構成員間における言語使用

Q3 　家族の者の間では通常、何語が使用されていますか。下の例を参考にしながら、各自が使用している言語を表3に記入して下さい。**なお複数の言語を使用している場合には、使用頻度が最も高い言語を〇で囲んで下さい。**

┌「英語」と「日本語」の両方を最も頻繁に使用している

（例）	母親	父親	子ども1	子ども2	子ども3	祖母	祖父
母親 ➡		英語	英語 日本語 フランス語	英語 日本語	日本語	日本語	

└「英語」を最も頻繁に使用している

表3							
話しかける人	話しかけられる人						
	母親	父親	子ども1	子ども2	子ども3	祖母	祖父
母親 ➡							
父親 ➡							
子ども1 ➡							
子ども2 ➡							
子ども3 ➡							
祖母 ➡							
祖父 ➡							

もしこの他に同居している**家族**がいれば、ここに追加記入して下さい。

Q4 家族の者同士で話をしている時、次の例のように言語を混合して使用するようなことがありますか。（例：It's めんどくさい, but I've got to do it.） それぞれ該当する□を1つだけ選び、Xの印を入れて下さい。

表4	全くしない	時々する	よくする	常にする	わからない
母親	□	□	□	□	□
父親	□	□	□	□	□
子ども1	□	□	□	□	□
子ども2	□	□	□	□	□
子ども3	□	□	□	□	□
祖母	□	□	□	□	□
祖父	□	□	□	□	□

もしこの他にも同居している家族がいれば、ここに追加記入して下さい。

B. 遊びにおける言語使用

Q5 子どもには、それぞれ（1）「日本語だけを話す友だち」、（2）「日本語を話さない友だち」、（3）「日本語とその他の言語も話す友だち」と遊ぶ機会がどのくらいありますか。項目ごとに該当する□を1つだけ選び、Xの印を入れて下さい。

表5	(1) 日本語だけを話す友だち	(2) 日本語を話さない友だち	(3) 日本語とその他の言語も話す友だち
子ども1	□ よくある □ 時々ある □ ほとんど／全くない	□ よくある □ 時々ある □ ほとんど／全くない	□ よくある □ 時々ある □ ほとんど／全くない
子ども2	□ よくある □ 時々ある □ ほとんど／全くない	□ よくある □ 時々ある □ ほとんど／全くない	□ よくある □ 時々ある □ ほとんど／全くない
子ども3	□ よくある □ 時々ある □ ほとんど／全くない	□ よくある □ 時々ある □ ほとんど／全くない	□ よくある □ 時々ある □ ほとんど／全くない

もしこの他にも子どもがいれば、ここに追加記入して下さい。

C. 学校の授業で用いられている言語

<u>Q6</u> 子どもの就学状況と、学校の授業で用いられている言語について記入して下さい。

1) 「就学状況」は該当するものを○で囲んで下さい。保育園や幼稚園に通っている場合も「就学中」として下さい。「就学中」の場合には「学校の種類」など、その他の質問にも答えて下さい。
2) 「学校の種類」とは、例えば「日本の公立学校」「日本の私立学校」「インターナショナル・スクール」「ミッション・スクール」などを指します。
3) 「学校区分」とは、「小学校」や「中学校」などの区分を指します。次の中から選んで下さい：

> 保育園、幼稚園、小学校、中学校、高等学校、短期大学、大学、
> 大学院、専門学校、その他（余白を用いて説明して下さい）

（例）子ども1	1) 就学状況	2) 学校の種類	3) 学校区分	学年	授業で用いられている言語
	就学前				
	就学中 ➡	日本の私立学校	中学校	2年	日本語
	就学終了				

表6	1) 就学状況	2) 学校の種類	3) 学校区分	学年	授業で用いられている言語
子ども1	就学前				
	就学中 ➡				
	就学終了				
子ども2	就学前				
	就学中 ➡				
	就学終了				
子ども3	就学前				
	就学中 ➡				
	就学終了				

もしこの他にも子どもがいれば、ここに追加記入して下さい。

D. 居住地

Q7 現在、次のどの地域に居住していますか。該当するものをA、Bそれぞれに1つずつ選び、□の中にXの印を入れて下さい。該当するものがない場合には、「その他」を選び、説明して下さい。

A： □ 都心部　　　□ 郊外　　　□ その他：＿＿＿＿＿＿＿＿＿＿

B： □ 住宅地　　　□ 農村地帯　　　□ 工場地帯　　　□ その他：＿＿＿＿＿＿＿＿

Q8 あなたの家族には、現在、居住している地域で、日本語以外の言語を話す人々と出会う機会がどのくらいありますか。

□ たくさんある　　　□ ある程度ある　　　□ ほとんどない　　　□ 全くない

Q9 近い将来、日本語以外の言語が話されている地域に引越す予定がありますか。

□ いいえ　　　□ はい ➡ そこでは主に何語が話されていますか：＿＿＿＿＿＿＿＿＿

III. バイリンガリズムに対する態度と認識

Q10 あなた方は、バイリンガルであること（ここでは「読む・書く」能力については考慮しなくても結構です）は有益であると考えていますか、それとも有害であると考えていますか。該当する□の中にXの印を入れ、なぜそう思うか理由を述べて下さい。

表7	なぜそう思いますか。
□ 有益	
□ 有害	
□ 両方	
□ どちらでもない	

Q11 あなた方二人の母語の組み合わせによるバイリンガルは、日本では一般にどのように受けとめられていると思いますか。該当する□の中にXの印を入れて下さい。

非常に肯定的	やや肯定的	中立	やや否定的	非常に否定的
□	□	□	□	□

Q12 別の言語の組み合わせによるバイリンガルも、日本において同じように受けとめられていると思いますか。該当する□の中にXの印を入れ、なぜそう思うか理由を述べて下さい。

表8	
□ はい	なぜそう思いますか。
□ いいえ	なぜそう思いますか。

Q13 子どもが日本人の友だちと一緒にいる時に、あなた方二人またはどちらか一方が、日本語以外の言語で子どもに話しかけ、そのために子どもから何か否定的な反応がかえってきたということがありますか。

表9
□ はい　　その時の状況、またその時あなた方はどう対応したか、説明して下さい。
□ いいえ　　何かコメントがあれば、自由に記入して下さい。

Q14 バイリンガル家族に生まれ育ったということで、子どもが何か好ましい、あるいは好ましくない経験をしたことがありますか。

表10
□ いいえ、親の知る限りでは、特にそのような経験はありません
□ はい

	□ 好ましい経験をしたことがあります	説明して下さい。
	□ 好ましくない経験をしたことがあります	説明して下さい。

IV. バイリンガリズムの奨励

Q15 あなた方は子どもをバイリンガル（ここでは「読む・書く」能力については考慮しなくても結構です）に育てようとしていますか。該当する□の中にXの印を入れ、各質問に答えて下さい。

表11	
□ はい	その理由を説明して下さい。 -- どのような方法でしていますか。
□ いいえ	その理由を説明して下さい。
□ その他	説明して下さい。

－－－－－－－－ ご協力どうもありがとうございました －－－－－－－－

このアンケート調査に加え、面接調査を実施したいと考えています。この面接調査にご協力下さるご家庭がありましたら、ご連絡先をお知らせ下さい。

プライバシーに関わる情報は一切、公には致しません

お名前： ＿＿＿＿＿＿＿＿＿＿＿＿＿＿＿＿＿＿＿＿＿＿＿＿＿

住所： ＿＿＿＿＿＿＿＿＿＿＿＿＿＿＿＿＿＿＿＿＿＿＿＿＿

電話番号： ＿＿＿＿＿＿＿＿＿＿＿＿＿＿＿＿＿＿＿＿＿＿＿＿＿

Appendix B

Table B1 Subjects' family structure

	Number of children			Family members					n (%)*	
Nuclear family										
n = 111 (94.1%)	1	M	F	C1	–	–	–	–	40	(33.9)
	2	M	F	C1	C2	–	–	–	58	(49.2)
	3	M	F	C1	C2	C3	–	–	13	(11.0)
Three-generation family										
n = 7 (5.9%)	1	M	F	C1	–	–	GM	–	1	(0.8)
	1	M	F	C1	–	–	GM	GF	1	(0.8)
	2	M	F	C1	C2	–	GM	–	2	(1.7)
	2	M	F	C1	C2	–	GM	GF	1	(0.8)
	3	M	F	C1	C2	C3	GM	–	1	(0.8)
	3	M	F	C1	C2	C3	–	GF	1	(0.8)
Total									118	(100.0)

M: mother   F: father   GM: grandmother   GF: grandfather
C1: first child (presence of sibling/s not specified)   C2: second child
C3: the third child

* The numbers in parentheses are percentages. The same notation will apply to all the following tables.

Table B2 Ages of parents

Age	20–29	30–39	40–49	50–59	Unknown	n
M	2 (1.7)	56 (47.5)	51 (43.2)	7 (5.9)	2 (1.7)	118 (100.0)
F	4 (3.4)	34 (28.8)	64 (54.2)	14 (11.9)	2 (1.7)	118 (100.0)

M: mother   F: father

Table B3 Ages of children

Age	3	4	5	6	7	8	9	10	11	12	13
C1	11	9	10	11	15	7	8	9	5	6	4
C2	12	12	7	5	10	3	7	4	5	4	1
C3	4	1	1	2	2	1	1	1	1	–	–
	27	22	18	18	27	11	16	14	11	10	5
	(12.9)	(10.5)	(8.6)	(8.6)	(12.9)	(5.3)	(7.7)	(6.7)	(5.3)	(4.8)	(2.4)

Age	14	15	16	17	19	20	21	23	28	
C1	5	7	5	2	–	1	2	–	1	subtotal = 118
C2	2	1	1	–	1	–	–	1	–	subtotal = 76
C3	–	–	1	–	–	–	–	–	–	subtotal = 15
	7	8	7	2	1	1	2	1	1	total = 209
	(3.3)	(3.8)	(3.3)	(1.0)	(0.5)	(0.5)	(1.0)	(0.5)	(0.5)	(100.0)

C1: first child (presence of sibling/s not specified)   C2: second child
C3: third child

Table B4 Ages of grandparents

Age	60–69	70–79	80–89	n
GM	2	4	–	6
GF	1	1	1	3

GM: grandmother   GF: grandfather

Table B5 Nationalities of parents, grandparents, and children

Nationality	M	F	C1	C2	C3	GM	GF	n
Single nationality	118	117	8	7	2	6	3	261
Japan	49	68	4	4	2	6	3	136
USA	58	39	3	2	–	–	–	102
Canada	1	2	–	–	–	–	–	3
Britain	6	8	–	–	–	–	–	14
Ireland	1	–	–	–	–	–	–	1
Australia	2	–	1	1	–	–	–	4
New Zealand	1	–	–	–	–	–	–	1
Dual nationality	0	1	109	68	13	0	0	191
Japan–USA	–	–	88	56	13	–	–	157
Japan–Canada	–	–	3	1	–	–	–	4
Japan–Britain	–	–	12	7	–	–	–	19
Japan–Ireland	–	–	1	–	–	–	–	1
Japan–Australia	–	–	3	3	–	–	–	6
Japan–Germany	–	–	1	1	–	–	–	2
Japan–New Zealand	–	–	1	–	–	–	–	1
Britain–Australia	–	1	–	–	–	–	–	1
Triple nationality	0	0	1	1	0	0	0	2
Japan–USA–Canada	–	–	1	1	–	–	–	2
Total	118	118	118	76	15	6	3	454

M: mother   F: father   GM: grandmother   GF: grandfather
C1: first child (presence of sibling/s not specified)   C2: second child
C3: third child

Table B6 Native languages of parents

M–Japanese/F–English		M–English/F–Japanese	
50	(42.4)	68	(57.6)

M: mother   F: father

Table B7 Native languages of children

	Japanese and English	*Japanese*	*English*	*Unknown*	*Total*
C1	75	36	6	1	118
C2	45	26	4	1	76
C3	6	8	–	1	15
	126 (60.3)	70 (33.5)	10 (4.8)	3 (1.4)	209 (100.0)

C1: first child (presence of sibling/s not specified)   C2: second child
C3: third child

Table B8 Experience living in non-Japanese environments

Languages spoken in the area(s)	*Area(s)*	*Length of stay: years*	*Number of families*
English	USA	13	1
English	USA	10	1
English+Chinese/Malay/ Indian/English	USA+Singapore	5+5	1
English	Canada	9	1
English	Canada	7	1
English	USA	6	1
English	USA	5	3
English	Canada	5	1
English+German	USA+Germany	2+3	1
German+English/Nepalese	Germany+Nepal	2+3	1
English	USA	3	1
English+Chinese	UK+China	1+2	1
English	USA	2	7
English	UK	2	1
English	Australia	2	1
English	USA	1	7
English	UK	1	1
German	Germany	1	1
Total			32

Table B9 Languages used by pJs, pEs and Cs

			Person addressed			C1-oc	C1-sib	C2	C3
			pL	pE	C				
s p e a k e r	pJ n=118	J		24 (20.3)	82 (39.2)	13	31	31	7
		E		54 (45.8)	12 (5.7)	4	3	5	–
		B		40 (33.9)	115 (55.0)	25	42	40	8
	pE n=118	J	12 (10.2)		9 (4.3)	–	4	4	1
		E	60 (50.8)		119 (56.9)	29	44	42	4
		B	46 (39.0)		81 (38.8)	13	28	30	10
	C $n_{(a-d)}$ = 209	J	106 (50.7)	32 (15.3)					
		E	14 (6.7)	89 (42.6)					
		B	89 (42.6)	88 (42.1)					
	C1-oc n_a=42	J	18	1					
		E	5	27					
		B	19	14					
	C1-sib n_b=76	J	40	(13)					
		E	3	(32)					
		B	33	(31)					
	C2 n_b=76	J	40	(14)					
		E	6	(26)					
		B	30	(36)					
	C3 n_d=15	J	8	(4)					
		E	–	(4)					
		B	7	(7)					

pJ: parent who is a native speaker of Japanese
pE: parent who is a native speaker of English
C: child C1-oc: first child, without sibling/s (i.e. only child)
C1-sib: first child, with sibling/s
C2: second child
C3: third child
J: Japanese
E: English
B: both Japanese and English
$n_{(a-d)}$: total number of children (i.e. $n_a + n_b + n_c + n_d$)
n_a: number of only children
n_b: number of first children with sibling/s
n_c: number of second children
n_d: number of third children

Table B10 Sibling language interaction

212 cases of sibling language interaction in total			Person addressed		
			C1-sib n = 76	C2 n = 76	C3 n = 15
s p e a k e r	C1-sib n = 76	J		33	8
		E		5	–
		B		38	7
	C2 n = 76	J	33		8
		E	5		–
		B	38		7
	C3 n = 15	J	8	8	
		E	–	–	
		B	7	7	

C1-sib: first child, with sibling/s   C2: second child   C3: third child
J: Japanese   E: English   B: both Japanese and English

Table B11 Frequency of code-mixing

	Never do it	Sometimes do it	Often do it	Always do it	Do not know	Unknown	n
pJ	39	60	17	2	–	–	118
pE	27	60	27	3	–	1	118
C1	31	57	24	3	1	2	118
C2	19	30	22	5	–	–	76
C3	5	4	4	2	–	–	15
GM	5	1	–	–	–	–	6
GF	2	1	–	–	–	–	3
Total	128 (28.2)	213 (46.9)	94 (20.7)	15 (3.3)	1 (0.2)	3 (0.7)	454 (100.0)

pJ: parent who is a native speaker of Japanese
pE: parent who is a native speaker of English
C1: first child (presence of sibling/s not specified)
C2: second child
C3: third child
GM: grandmother
GF: grandfather

Table B12 Play opportunities, sorted by playmate language group

| | **Children who speak only Japanese** | | | | |
	often	*sometimes*	*hardly ever/never*	*unknown*	*n*
C1	107	8	2	1	118
C2	67	6	2	1	76
C3	15	–	–	–	15
Total	189 (90.4)	14 (6.7)	4 (1.9)	2 (1.0)	209 (100.0)

| | **Children who do not speak Japanese** | | | | |
	often	*sometimes*	*hardly ever/never*	*unknown*	*n*
C1	14	35	67	2	118
C2	5	17	52	2	76
C3	–	4	10	1	15
Total	19 (9.1)	56 (26.8)	129 (61.7)	5 (2.4)	209 (100.0)

| | **Children who speak both Japanese and an/other language/s** | | | | |
	often	*sometimes*	*hardly ever/never*	*unknown*	*n*
C1	29	52	36	1	118
C2	13	34	26	3	76
C3	1	8	6	–	15
Total	43 (20.6)	94 (45.0)	68 (32.5)	4 (1.9)	209 (100.0)

C1: first child (presence of sibling/s not specified)   C2: second child
C3: third child

Table B13 School enrollment

	Not yet in school	*In school now*	*Already out of school*	*n*
C1	4	113	1	118
C2	6	70	–	76
C3	1	14	–	15
Total	11 (5.3)	197 (94.3)	1 (0.5)	209 (100.0)

C1: first child (presence of sibling/s not specified)   C2: second child
C3: third child

Table B14 Level of school

	P	K	E	JH	SH	C/U	O	n
C1	10	19	51	16	12	3	2	113
C2	8	17	34	6	2	1	2	70
C3	3	3	7	–	1	–	–	14
Total	21	39	92	22	15	4	4	197
	(10.7)	(19.8)	(46.7)	(11.2)	(7.6)	(2.0)	(2.0)	(100.0)

P = preschool   K = kindergarten E = elementary school   JH = junior high
school   SH = senior high school   C/U = college/university   O = other
C1: first child (presence of sibling/s not specified)   C2: second child
C3: third child

Table B15 Type of school

	Japanese public school	Japanese private school	International school	Others	Unknown	n
C1	57	32	14	4	6	113
C2	39	17	5	2	7	70
C3	9	3	1	–	1	14
Total	105 (53.3)	52 (26.4)	20 (10.2)	6 (3.0)	14 (7.1)	197 (100.0)

C1: first child (presence of sibling/s not specified)   C2: second child
C3: third child

Table B16 Medium of instruction

	One language		Two languages			
	Japanese	English	Japanese– English	Japanese– Korean	Unknown	n
C1	92	17	2	1	1	113
C2	60	7	3	–	–	70
C3	13	1	–	–	–	14
Total	165 (83.8)	25 (12.7)	5 (2.5)	1 (0.5)	1 (0.5)	197 (100.0)

C1: first child (presence of sibling/s not specified)   C2: second child
C3: third child

Table B17 Location of residence

	Inner city	Suburb	Other	Unknown	n
residential	11	57	6	6	80 (67.8)
farming	–	4	3	2	9 (7.6)
factory	–	–	–	–	–
other	1	2	2	–	5 (4.2)
unknown	8	15	–	1	24 (20.3)
n	20 (16.9)	78 (66.1)	11 (9.3)	9 (7.6)	118(100.0)

Table B18 Opportunities for meeting non-Japanese speakers

Many	Some	Few	None	Unknown	Total
21 P	162	162			
(17.8)	43 (36.4)	44 (37.3)	8 (6.8)	2 (1.7)	118 (100.0)

Table B19 Plan to move to non-Japanese-speaking areas

No	Yes	Unknown	Total
101 (85.6)	13 (11.0)	4 (3.4)	118 (100.0)

Table B20 Attitudes towards bilingualism

Beneficial	Detrimental	Both	Neither	Total
104 (88.1)	–	12 (10.2)	2 (1.7)	118 (100.0)

Table B21 Assessment of Japanese perception of J–E bilinguals

Very positive	Somewhat positive	Neutral	Somewhat negative	Very negative	Unknown	Total
78 (66.1)	33 (28.0)	2 (1.7)	3 (2.5)	–	2 (1.7)	118 (100.0)

J–E bilinguals: Japanese–English bilinguals

Table B22 Assessment of Japanese perception of language combinations other than J–E

Same	*Different*	*Unknown*	*Total*
33 (28.0)	75 (63.6)	10 (8.5)	118 (100.0)

J: Japanese   E: English

Table B23 Children's negative reaction to being addressed in English

Yes	*No*	*Unknown*	*Total*
44 (37.3)	72 (61.0)	2 (1.7)	118 (100.0)

Table B24 Specific experiences

	Yes				
No	*Desirable*	*Undesirable*	*Both*	*Unknown*	*Total*
32 (27.1)	21 (17.8)	17 (14.4)	47 (39.8)	1 (0.8)	118 (100.0)

Table B25 Promotion of bilingualism

Yes	*No*	*Other*	*Unknown*	*Total*
106 (89.8)	6 (5.1)	5 (4.2)	1 (0.8)	118 (100.0)

Table B26 Language use between every pair of interlocutors in the subject group

INT-1 INT-2	Total Monolingual Use		Collective Bilingual Use		Partial Bilingual Use J-oriented		Partial Bilingual Use E-oriented		Total Bilingual Use	
	Type 1 J J	Type 2 E E	Type 3 J E	Type 4 E J	Type 5 J B	Type 6 B J	Type 7 E B	Type 8 B E	Type 9 B B	n
pJ pE	12 (10.2)	54 (45.8)	4 (3.4)		8 (6.8)			2 (1.7)	38 (32.2)	118 (100.0)
pJ C	79 (37.8)	11 (5.3)	–	–	3 (1.4)	27 (12.9)	1 (0.5)	3 (1.4)	85 (40.7)	209 (100.0)
pJ C1-oc	12	4	–	–	1	6	–	1	18	42
pJ C1-sib/C2/C3	67	7	–	–	2	21	1	2	67	167

pE / C	9 (4.3)	82 (39.2)	–	8 (3.8)	–	15 (7.2)	29 (13.9)	7 (3.3)	59 (28.2)	209 (100.0)
pE / C1-oc	–	23	–	1	–	–	5	4	9	42
pE / C1-sib/C2/C3	9	59	–	7	–	15	24	3	50	167
C / C	48 (45.3)	5 (4.7)	–	–	1 (0.9)	1 (0.9)	–	–	51 (48.1)	106 (100.0)
C / C1-sib	32	5	–	–	1	1	–	–	37	76
C / C2	8	–	–	–	–	–	–	–	7	15
C / C3	8	–	–	–	–	–	–	–	7	15

INT-1: interlocutor 1   INT-2: interlocutor 2
pJ: parent who is a native speaker of Japanese   pE: parent who is a native speaker of English
C: child   C1-oc: first child (presence of sibling/s not specified)   C1-sib: first child, with sibling/s
C2: second child   C3: third child   C1-sib/C2/C3 : all children with sibling/s
J: Japanese   E: English   B: both Japanese and English

Index

academic advantages 23, 29
amount of exposure to languages 11, 125
Appel, R. 12, 61, 97
Asians 21, 35, 73
attitudes 16f, 20, 49, 107
– towards bilingualism 2, 16f, 20, 47ff, 69, 86, 129
– towards differences 83
– towards English 109
– towards languages 16f, 20, 48
– towards trilingualism 10
audio cassettes 84

Bain, B. 35, 99
Baker, C. 38
Bayley, R. 94
Bellin, W. 15
bicultural/biculturalism 78f, 82, 84, 87
bilingual/bilinguals 1, 4, 7f, 11, 15-17, 26, 37f, 41f, 46, 49, 56, 61, 69f, 74, 76ff, 99, 105, 107, 110, 113, 127, 129f
– active bilinguals 1, 3, 5, 29, 32, 112
– active bilingual acquisition/development 6, 99f, 127
– bilingual ability/abilities 1, 3, 10, 69f, 78f, 114, 124, 130
– bilingual child-rearing 48, 50, 82f, 94, 96, 103, 114, 121, 124, 130
– bilingual competence 7, 99
– bilingual development 2, 4ff, 12, 16, 18, 20, 26, 28, 49, 99
– bilingual families 1, 38f, 79
– bilingual language acquisition 25
– bilingual language use 85
– bilingual proficiency 5, 28f, 31ff, 100
– bilingual school 14
– perception of bilinguals 71ff
– balanced bilingual 116
– productive bilingual 3

– simultaneous bilinguals 8
bilingualism 2, 4, 9ff, 16, 21, 30, 37ff, 46, 49, 69ff, 81ff, 110, 112, 129f
– active bilingualism 5ff, 17, 28ff, 99, 127
– passive bilingualism 5f, 28ff, 127
– perception of bilingualism 2, 47ff, 69ff, 94ff, 103
– promotion of bilingualism 2, 5, 32f, 47ff, 81, 99
– in interlingual families 4
Billings, M. 28f, 35, 99
biracial 79
Blanc, M. H. A. 38
bullying 80
Byram, M. 49

Celce-Murcia, M. 4
character-building 69f, 81f, 86f
child-centered interactional style 5
children who need supplemental
    Japanese language instruction 22f
Clyne, M. 13, 20, 38, 40
code-mixing 7, 61f, 86
– code-switching 7f, 17, 61, 86, 116
– language mixing 7ff, 20
cognitive development 69f, 81, 86f
Collective Bilingual Use 88, 90f, 105
conducive linguistic input 5
conflicting identities 70
consistent adherence 6
core values 12f, 20
cross-cultural understanding 69f, 81, 86f
cross-generational interactions 18
Crystal, D. 3, 41
cultural
– and societal norms 15, 20
– distance 13
– heritage 121
Cummins, J. 97

166